Dear 20-Something

Ronni Morgan

All rights reserved. No part of this book may be reproduced or utilized in any form or by any means, electronic or mechanical, including photocopying, recording or by any information storage or retrieval system, without permission in writing from the Publisher. Published by Culturatti Ink in partnership with The Mold Agency. Inquiries should be emailed to adam@themoldagency.com.

Find out more about Ronni at:
www.BreakUpWithRonni.com.

Publishing Consulting by Erika Parsons.

Creative Direction by The Mold Agency.

Copyright © 2017 by Ronni Morgan

ISBN: 978-0-692-06343-9

Library of Congress Control Number: 2018940316

Printed in the United States of America.

First Printing: 2018

The next time you hear from me, it will be to tell you, what is undeniably, one of the best breakup stories you'll ever hear. It will be to chronicle for you how I took the immense amount of pain I was in, and turned it into the most powerful, life-altering journey of my life. You'll laugh, you'll cry, you'll be ready to kick my ex square in the face, and then you'll realize he is what matters least about the entire story. Because this is a story about being victorious. It's about breaking up, not only with a partner, but with the old versions of myself that were holding me back.

Ronni

Table of Contents

Forward 5
Preface 8
First Jobs, Pity Parties & An Italian Adventure 13
    Pennies in a Jar 14
    Fortune Sides with She Who Dares 18
    My Yawn-inducing Life 20
    Scuffle in Paris 21
    Big Risks, Big Rewards 24
Doers Gotta Do 33
    The Shit-Show Begins 35
    Are You a Doer? 36
    7 Steps to Becoming a Doer 37
    The End of the Shit-Show...Maybe 42
    Bosses Shouldn't Equal Best Friends 43
    5 Reasons Why NOT to Befriend Your Boss 45
    A Giant Sigh of Relief 47
    Put Your Best Face Forward 50
    Social Media & The Job Hunt 101 51
    We Are Millennials, Hear Us Roar 54
    Job Hunt Check List 57
Finding Your Health 63
    Weird, Unhealthy Trends 66
    Bikini Bridges and Other Skinny Nonsense 69
    2 or 22, Happy Isn't a Number 70
    What is Healthy 71
    You Are What You Eat 72
    Running for My Life 80
    Drop It Like A Squat 82
    Weight Lifting to the Rescue 86
    Dear Self, You're Pretty Damn Awesome 88
It's Overrated Till It's Not 93
    Love Yourself First 94
    6 Steps to Loving Yourself 95
    Love Is...Love Isn't 99

How to Know You've Met the Right One 99
The Art of Modern Dating 100
Online Dating Do's and Don'ts 102
Pursuing a Love Interest 104
Quirky Rituals = Healthy Couples 107
Should I Stay Or Should I Go? 110
When to Let Go—The Checklist 111
Finding Your Love Tribe 115
6 Steps to Creating Your Tribe 118
19 Times Your Tribe Will Save The Day 124
Career Vs. Passion 131
7 Ways to Know You've Found Your Passion 136
What Does It Take To Build on Your Passion? 137
What Does Working in a Job Feel Like 137
What Is Your Why 141
Education: A Big Grey Area 145
Test The Waters 150
Forge Ahead—The Path of Service 151
Grab Your Passport and Ship Out 153
For the Love Of Money 157
Starting Off on the Right Foot 159
I Have a Grown-Up Job. Now What? 162
A Few Final Pointers 170
Living Fearlessly 173
11 Times You've Been Afraid and Didn't Know It ... 176
I'm Attached to My Arms, Not My Ideas 182
6 Ideals Worth Changing 184
Ego vs. Higher Self 189
You Are What You Think 191
5 Steps To Zen 191
Know What You Want? Manifest That Shit 200
Peace Out 206
So, This is Where I Leave You 209

Preface

The idea to write this book came about two years before I started writing it. I was smack dab in the middle of my 20s and frustrated as hell. I felt like I was floundering. I constantly felt behind. Behind what exactly? Everything and everyone. It felt like everyone was privy to some key piece of information that told them how to dominate their 20s that I wasn't. Then I realized, most of my 20-something friends felt the same way. We were all feeling like children trapped in adult bodies. Adulting? How the hell does anyone do this? When I mentioned this to my friends, who were long since out of their 20s, they cringed and agreed: being in your 20s actually sucks a lot.

Why didn't anyone warn us? Couldn't someone have given us a heads up? As a good friend of mine once said, it truly is the best of times, and worst of times.

I wrote this book to give you a heads up. The one I wish I'd had, before I learned a lot of lessons the hard way. You're either about to be, or are right in the middle of traversing some seriously rocky landscapes of self-discovery and personal evolution. I hope you find solace as you read this book and realize you're not alone, and what you're going through isn't only normal, but to be expected.

We're going to cover a lot of important topics together in this book. Everything from travel, love and friendship, to finding your passions, how to avoid getting taken advantage of, and living courageously. We spend a lot of time feeling alone in our 20s. But, the truth is, we all feel lost. My goal in writing this, is to help you feel a little less lost, and a lot less alone.

This book marks the end of my 20-something era. An ending that was marked with an epic split from the man I thought I was going to marry, a few bonus heartbreaks, dismantling many layers of self-doubt, chucking my career to travel the world, and finally deciding to take control of rewriting my own story. Hey, I don't do anything half way. I needed a grande finale that rivaled all finales to send me off into the next decade.

I hope this book will help you on your journey to self-actualization. I hope it helps you realize your innate ability to write your own story, and create your own reality. I hope it shows you that there's no singular way to succeed in life. You know more than you think you do. I hope this helps you learn to trust yourself.

I can't wait to hear from you once you're done reading this love letter.

Cheers to us, 20-Somethings.

Chapter One
FIRST JOBS, PITY PARTIES, & AN ITALIAN ADVENTURE

Hey, 20-Something, how are things? I'm super pumped that you've decided to pick up this little number I've written. I hope you'll get as much joy out of reading it as I have out of writing it. This is a work of love. I wrote it for everybody who's already been through this tumultuous decade and rocked it; for everybody who's about to embark on the journey; and for those who are right in the thick of it. Hold on tight: it's going to be a wild ride. We're about to dive head-first into some pretty intense stuff, but let's face it, intense is the name of the game for us 20-somethings. Life is about to kick your ass, repeatedly. It will fluff you up for a while and make you think you're really dominating this whole 20s thing, only to turn around and kick you in the ass again. It's like one of those Sour Patch Kids commercials: it's sweet, then it's sour, repeat. Fear not! I'm going to help you learn how to make life your bitch. It's time to put on your big girl panties*, and learn how to do some ass kicking of your own! Suit up, soldier. We've got a lot to cover and adventures to be had!

* Big Girl Panties:
(adj) To be strong, grow up, and be an adult.

Pennies in a Jar

At age 22, I was standing at the edge of a cliff; I had some major life changes to make. My job teaching at a cosmetology school was no longer adding to my happiness, and was instead causing me all kinds of stress. I loved my co-workers and my students, but the institute politics left me feeling defeated and constantly drained.

On top of the working-girl blues, I broke up with my boyfriend of two years. Let's call him "Dan." Dan was great. He was charming, dorky and silly. We had loads of fun together, but our relationship lacked depth. When he moved away after graduating college, we became a long-distance couple. I'm here to tell you, long-distance is rough; it will test even the strongest of people. As our lives started spinning off into new and separate directions, my love for him changed. We didn't see each other enough to do anything about it, so we fizzled out. Maybe I could've followed him to New York, but that didn't feel like the right choice. For the sake of my own happiness, I had to do what was best for me.

I needed a vacation bad, but I was flat broke. For over a year, I desperately tried to save money so I could go to Italy to visit my brother, Anthony, and my sister-in-law, Maria, who happen to be two of my best friends. They understand me better than most people do, and our sense of humor is nearly identical. I knew that being in the company of such kindred souls in Italy, the country of love and lovely cuisine, was just what I needed to turn up the heat on my life. But, somehow things just kept coming up. Any meager amount of money I managed to save would seem to disappear. Needless to say, I frequently had pity parties back then.

Oh, woe is me, life is so hard.

I'm so poor, I'm never going to go anywhere!

What is my life?

Blah, blah, blah.

#MillennialProblems

I have to admit that I just hadn't made saving money as high of a priority as I could have back then. It was a mistake that kept me stagnant, stuck, and unable to lead the kind of life I wanted to live. Anyway, once I stopped playing the victim, HOORAY! I was finally able to save enough to fly to Italy. It's funny how things work out once you stop wallowing in self-pity. **Have you found yourself wallowing in self-pity and playing the victim?** Don't worry, I've got some steps to help you break the cycle:

1. Lose the victim attitude.

2. Take responsibility for your life choices. No one forced you to make the choices you've made. For whatever reason, you made them, so suck it up buttercup.

3. Check your level of broke-ness. Do you have a roof over your head? Are the lights on? Did you eat at least one substantial meal today? If you've answered yes to these, you're not broke, you're just "Millennial broke," and we can work with that.

4. Look for reasons to be grateful for your life. The more gratitude you have, the better life will become.

* Millennial Broke:
(verb)

When you have just enough money to cover your rent, living expenses, student loan payment, that $12 cocktail at the bar last weekend (Okay, both cocktails), and a new outfit...but are crossing your fingers that you don't overdraft your account before you get paid again. Your inability to save has you feeling like a broke victim of being a 20-30 something in a crap economy.

Fortune Sides with She Who Dares

That trip to Italy changed my life. I was traveling weeks at a time for work prior to that vacation, so I was accustomed to flying alone. But flying across the world alone? Well, that proved to be a terrifying and thrilling cocktail of self-discovery. Maneuvering foreign airports, with no means of communication, was a little unnerving. Once I left American soil, I no longer had the use of my cell phone—my lifeline—the single most important tool in my ability to navigate the world. I just kept repeating to myself, What's the worst that can happen? I have my boarding passes, and I'm a smart girl. I've got this.

I was on my own and it was exhilarating! I could've been anywhere, doing anything, and no one would've been the wiser. It was in that moment that I truly learned how fantastic it is to disconnect. Shut off your phone sometimes, 20-Something, and see the world anew! Have experiences without updating everyone immediately. Keep them to yourself for a while.

I was giddy like a child on Christmas Eve. Every single thing about that trip was magical for me because it was new and exciting. Whenever I think back on that adventure, I am filled with the same warmth and happiness. I fell in love with Italy and everything about it. I fell in love with the way I felt in Italy: excited, free, and intrigued. It was the most extraordinary two weeks of my life.

The last couple of days of that trip, Anthony and Maria kept dropping subtle hints that I should stay. I know now that they were holding back from coming right out and asking, because they didn't want to pressure me. I was holding back because I was afraid to say out loud that I hated my life back home and needed a change. The idea of dropping everything and moving to Italy seemed way riskier than anything I could accomplish. I had never done anything so bold.

My Yawn-inducing Life...

As my vacation days dwindled and I was nearing my return home, I became filled with dread. I wasn't happy to be going back to my monotonous life. I felt like I had finally awakened after sleepwalking for eons. Going back to my "normal" life was going to be uncomfortable. It was like trying to fit into an old pair of pants I had outgrown. I had changed. And there I was, getting ready to leave the greatest place I had ever known, to head back to my small, unfulfilling life.

Every mile I put between Italy and myself was a little heavier weight on my shoulders. I knew I needed to make a change, but fear kept putting doubt in the back of my mind, causing me to question whether I was capable of such a ballsy move.

Scuffle in Paris

My flight from Italy to Paris was late, but my connecting flight from Paris back to the U.S. was right on time. Figures! I found an airport employee who told me I missed my connection and sent me to a help desk. I stood at the help desk for probably 15 minutes before a woman declared that in fact I had NOT missed my flight, and I'd better run. I hauled ass...hoping and praying I could somehow make it to the gate in time. I set off on a clumsy half-run, half-sprint through that enormous airport wearing those ridiculous Reebok shoes that are supposed to tone your thighs as you walk (three months and my thighs were still jiggling!). My gigantic book bag was furiously bouncing up and down, left and right, as I ran, throwing off my already questionable balance. Not to mention, I was sweating harder than Janet Jackson during Nipplegate 2004.

Long story short, another 15 minutes, a tram ride, and a customs check later, I could finally see my gate. They almost didn't let me on the plane, and had actually given my seat away. The gate attendant, who must've seen the look of smoldering rage and desperation on my face, gave me back my seat.

I was the last person to board the plane. We're talking jumbo jet. Every seat on that beast was full, and here I showed up, all sweaty and winded, trying to look cool as I searched for space in an overhead bin. I started calmly shifting around some ill-placed items (seriously, who put that straw fedora there?), when I heard someone behind me getting huffy. I ignored him, hoping he'd think better than to cross me. And then it happened: I heard him clear his throat loudly and then blurt, "Ma'am! Ma'am! That's my camera bag you're moving!" but I remained calm. Without turning around, I said, "Well sir, maybe if you moved this hat you've decided to store up here, there would be room for my bag." He responded, "Well, maybe if you got to the gate on time, there would be room for your bag."

Oh no, he didn't! Was he for real? Could he not see my sweat-soaked face and the damp hair matted to my forehead? I put up my pointer finger in notorious "wait one minute" fashion and slowly turned around.

That's when I first laid eyes on him—that typical yuppie-looking, entitled 30-something and his equally yuppie wife. UGH! My disdain grew and I said, "Excuse me! I clearly didn't just stroll on here all willy-nilly from a jaunt at the pub, sir. I suggest you turn back around and mind your own business before I take this hat of yours and..."

"Miss? Miss? I can fit your bag over here, no problem," interrupted the flight attendant. At that point, the entire coach section of the plane was straining their necks to watch the whole exchange. I decided in that moment it was best if I just let it go, and thanked the flight attendant. I handed her my bag, gave that obnoxious yuppie one final death glare, and then took my seat.

I shot daggers into the back of that man's head. Who did he think he was? The level of douchebaggery was astounding! They even had matching neck pillows, eye covers, and slippers. Slippers! As if that weren't lame enough, they had tiny toothbrushes they used at least three times during the flight. Okay, maybe I wished I had thought of that, too, after eating that disgusting plane food, but that's not the point here. Finally, to add insult to injury, they were occupying three—count them: THREE—overhead bins!

Eventually, after I felt I had wished him enough bad karma to last a lifetime, I put in my earbuds and got back to thinking about my life.

Big Risks, Big Rewards

I silenced my fears and started entertaining the thought of moving to Italy. What would it take? What would I have to do? As I sat in the Atlanta airport waiting to board my final flight home, I called my mom to talk everything over. I'd have to quit my job and leave behind my steady salary and health benefits. I couldn't just leave my roommate with the whole lease and rent payment, so I'd have to find someone to take over my share. I'd need extra money, so I would have to sell the majority of my things. All these tasks were big, but after talking them over with Mom, they were feeling much less overwhelming. I hung up my phone after saying I'd continue to think about it, but deep down, I knew the decision was already made.

Two weeks later, every task on my list was complete. Miraculously, I managed to find a roommate to take my place at the apartment. That was the most difficult part of the equation. Thank God for Craigslist, and thank God the applicant was normal and not some sociopathic serial killer. She and my roommate ended up being great friends.

Two months later, the second week of January 2011, I would be boarding a plane with nothing but a backpack and one suitcase, and flying back to my Zen place.

During those long two months leading up to my big adventure, I was nervous. So many people told me how amazed they were—that they could never take such a big leap, and they wished they were as adventurous or strong. I think the envy from others was probably about the balls it took to make such a big leap, more than anything. There would always be time to get a new job. I'd still need to make student loan payments while I was gone, and for that, I had managed to save a nice little nest egg during those last two months, so I wasn't worried. Life is about taking risks. The greater the risk, the greater the reward. If I wanted to talk myself out of going, I could've come up with a hundred reasons. If I were going to wait until I was financially ready, I never would've gone. It was now or never.

When I left the States, there was a blizzard that caused my flight to be rerouted. When I arrived in Naples, Italy, it was 65 degrees and sunny. I stepped off the plane, closed my eyes, took in a deep breath of Italian air and lifted my face to the sky. Thank you for bringing me here, I said to myself. Thank you for doing this.

I was able to stay for three months. There weren't as many exciting activities as my first trip to Italy. Most of that time was spent in self-reflection or doing nothing at all. I've never been good with idle time. I like to be active and on the go, and suddenly that wasn't an option. My brother was working most days.

We only had one car and we didn't live within walking distance to anything. So, in an attempt to stay busy, I read 15 books, played around on the computer, and listened to Adele on repeat, only stopping for intermittent Law & Order SVU marathons. Maria and I took lots of walks around the neighborhood and did Insanity workout DVDs in the afternoons. Occasionally someone would book my hair services. We went out to dinner often and ran various errands. Most nights, we watched movies in the living room, and I wrote until my eyes crossed.

We did a fair amount of traveling on the weekends, taking leisurely road trips to beautiful places like Florence, Rome, the Amalfi coast, and Capri. Watching the Italian landscapes go by was mesmerizing. I daydreamed during those car rides, thinking deeply about my life and the people in it, and what I wanted my world to look like. Sometimes I didn't think at all: I was just present. I'd close my eyes and breathe in the Italian air. Everything took my breath away. Every moment spent immersed in Italian culture brought me closer to being the person I am today.

Once I adjusted to the idle time, I realized how important it was that I was forced to be still. Traveling constantly wasn't the point and maybe would've been just another distraction. Spending days lounging around the house with Maria, singing loudly and laughing freely were healing to my soul. Before moving to Italy I didn't take time to be still, to have quiet time or little silly moments. I was constantly pushing myself toward the next thing rather than slowing down to enjoy the here and now. I took myself and my life so seriously. Being in Italy showed me what it really meant to be in the present. Was I going to spend what precious time I had there worrying about what would happen when I got home, or what people were thinking about me? I sure as hell was not. Italy brought on a childlike wonder that had been missing for years. I allowed my wonderment to show. I allowed the child in me to come alive, and doing this allowed parts of me to shine that before had started fading away. I danced in the streets of Cinque Terre, just because I wanted to. There was so much love and excitement flowing through me that I just needed to dance about it! Amazingly, no one looked at me like I was crazy. People smiled and clapped along with me. It was awesome. There was no shortage of laughter—deep, satisfying laughter that penetrated my soul. I was growing more confident in myself all the time.

Before leaving home for this adventure, I was waiting for someone or something to come along and force me out of my own misery. I thought something would change if I just kept trudging along... doing what I was supposed to be doing, working, paying rent, paying student loans. I thought that maybe one day something exciting would happen and life would be better. It's not true. It won't happen. You'll work, you'll pay and eventually you'll die. Luckily, I realized that if I don't create opportunities for myself, nothing will ever happen. Before Italy, I had just been floating, coasting, half-asleep. I was the only one who could shake myself awake.

Because of those three blissful months in Italy—those three life-changing months—I became a more interesting person, someone who takes risks. Handling whatever was going to happen next in my life would be a breeze, because I did what so many people considered impossible.

Choosing to leave everything familiar behind and throw myself into this adventure was the single greatest decision I had ever made. It was pivotal. I encourage you to do the same thing. Maybe your adventure won't be identical to mine, but try to force yourself out of your comfortable environment and become immersed in the unfamiliar, the unknown. How can you truly understand how the world works if you don't get out and experience it? You have to leave home and just go. See how people live in other cultures. My Italian experience taught me to be courageous. It taught me that I can do anything. If I could do that, with all of my self-doubt and insecurities, then you can, too. Anything is possible if you want it badly enough. Nothing is out of your reach. The confines of our minds are the heaviest chains we carry. Only we can cut them loose. Only we can free ourselves. Take a chance and learn to trust yourself. Your future self will thank you.

Chapter Two
DOERS GOTTA DO

"When someone tells me, "no," it doesn't mean I can't do it, it simply means I can't do it with them."
-Karen E. Quinones Miller

Eventually I came home. Culture shock was real, and an entirely new struggle began. I moved back in with my parents. I didn't know what my end game was. I had no intention of making this situation permanent, but I had no clue where to go or what to do next. How do I follow up something as huge as a solo international expedition? What does the next chapter even look like compared to that?

Maybe people expected me to do crazy awesome things, and continue taking risks that they were to afraid to take. I had set a standard and I had to keep it up. I wish my present-day self could go tap my previous self on the shoulder and say: "Excuse me, self, no one gives a damn what you're doing. Just be happy."

I began making poor decisions right away. I didn't realize they were poor at the time, but you know, hindsight and all that. I should've taken the time to figure out what I was looking for career wise. I should've made lists and set goals. I didn't do any of that. I had one major thought about which salon I chose; I needed to start making money now.

You're going to see me address, "finding your why" several times throughout this book. That's because it's imperative that you know the reason behind the actions you're taking. I didn't have anyone helping me slow down my thought process and ask, "but Ronni, what is the why?"

I was blindly going on interviews, hoping for nothing more than getting hired.

The Shit-Show Begins

We'll call the salon in my hometown, Salon A. I viewed my newly found employment there as a real victory. It wasn't, for several reasons:

1. The environment was toxic. The relationships between my boss and fellow stylists was tumultuous, shallow and caddy.
2. I was expected to do a lot of work that took me away from what was important; building a clientele and becoming a better stylist.
3. My boss offered no positive feedback or support.
4. The opportunities for growth were non-existent.
5. My boss was resistant to change.

Pro Tip *If during your interview, your prospective boss divulges to you that he is a lousy boss, believe him.*

I am a natural doer. I hate wasted energy and time. I spent a lot of time at Salon A with little opportunity to do anything that mattered. All the grunt work wasn't helping me gain any traction. Does this wasted time and energy sound familiar to you? Back then I was an amateur doer; I didn't know how to use this trait productively. You can be the hardest working person at the office, but if you're directionless, you'll waste days, weeks, and then oh snap, a year has gone by. If you're no further along than you were 12 months ago, you may not be using your time as productively as you could. Successful people act with purpose.

Are You a Doer?

A doer is a self-motived queen who finds what she wants and goes after it relentlessly. She doesn't need anyone to hold her hand. She identifies obstacles and creates solutions for overcoming them. She doesn't dwell on what she's lacking. She focuses on the resources she already has. She recognizes her shortcomings and seeks out the right people to mentor her. She is a beast at getting what she wants.

7 Steps to Becoming a Doer: Don't just talk about it, be about it.

1. **Set Your Objectives.**
   - What are you passionate about?
   - What qualities are you looking for in an employer?

2. **Set Goals.**
   - It's important to have a long-term goal. Without one, you are directionless. It's okay if your goal changes, likely it will. Set one anyway, and be intentional about it.

   - Next, set a few short-term goals that will help you accomplish the Big Kahuna. If you don't know what steps to take, ask someone who is in the same field for guidance.

3. **Know Yourself and Embrace Your Strengths and Weaknesses.**
   - Determine what your strengths are and play into them. We always do our best work when it's something we do well.

   - Respect your weaknesses and figure out ways to work through them (delegate the task to someone else, find a coach, etc).

   - Understand your work habits. What works/doesn't work for you? If you know you don't work well in a stuffy office, then don't settle for a stuffy office, even if they offer you the job.

   - Find your "rabbit." That is, someone who is ahead of you on the path. Instead of being frustrated and feeling, "behind," use them as motivation to keep pushing yourself forward.

4. **Keep Tabs on Your Productivity.**
   - Make "to-do" lists and prioritize what needs to be done. These lists should be on a monthly, weekly, and daily basis. Prioritizing tasks this way will ensure you get things done on time.
   - Check things off your list to gage if you're working productively.

5. **Figure Out How to Work Smarter, Not Harder.**
   - Why do something in eight hours when you could do it in four? Always be vigilant of your time and how you're working. Are you spending too much time on a task because you don't know how to do it efficiently? Have regular check-ins with yourself and always be on the lookout for smarter ways to do what you're doing.

6. **Reward Yourself.**
   - When you've checked all the boxes on your to-do list for the week, do something nice for yourself. Rewards will keep you motivated.
   - When you're close to reaching a major goal, plan something big for yourself. Sometimes when you're nearing the end of a months, or year long project it can be hard to stay focused. For big goals, I reward myself with a new tattoo, or a vacation. Choose whatever tickles your fancy and lights a fire under your ass.

7. **Surround Yourself with Other Doers.**
   - Nothing is more imperative to a doer than surrounding herself with other motivated, like-minded doers. Surround yourself with other people who are doing big things. Successful businessman, Jim Rohn once said, "you are the average of the five people you spend the most time with." Who are your five and what are they doing?

I was not surrounded by like-minded people. My co-workers weren't bad people, but they weren't my people. Their lives were not a reflection of what I wanted my life to be. I needed to spend time with people who challenged me to be better and get my shit together. Not only did I not have my shit together, but I felt that I was veering far off any path I wanted to been on. It was the, get-wified-up-and-pop-out-a-kid, path. Followed by the, work-behind-the-chair-until-your-fingers-crinkle-up-with-arthritis-and-you-can-barely-walk-anymore, path.

I wasn't being challenged in a productive way. I knew I wasn't growing anything but resentful at Salon A. After what still stands as the longest year and a half of my life, I left. I walked away with having gained one significant new talent; the ability to swallow my words, paste a fake smile on my face, and not slap anyone. I'll admit, is has proven handy in many situations. My boss was right, he was a lousy boss, bless his heart.

The End of the Shit Show...Maybe?

When I was searching for my next salon I did it with a hope, a prayer, and a lot of website stalking. When I found my next salon's website, I knew it was the one. We'll call this Salon B. According to their website, they took cabin retreats together. They even looked like they were enjoying each other! The owner had cool hair and even cooler tattoos. The stylists all looked incredibly unique. The salon was modern and chic, and looked nothing like most salons in the Mid-west. These were my people. This was my place. I could feel it.

Do your research 20-Something! Everyone is on social media these days. Find out who works at your prospective place of employment. Get a feel for who they are. Let's face it, if someone doesn't have a strong web presence, they are simply not to be trusted.

After a few exchanged emails I set up a time and drove two hours south to Indianapolis for an interview with the owner. I was right, she was rad. The salon was as awesome as I thought it was going to be. She offered me the job that day and I said yes.

For a while, working at Salon B was exactly what I needed. My boss was an incredible educator. My skills improved leaps and bounds; I went from simply "doing hair" to being an artist. She was teaching me how to be confident behind the chair; how to take control and own my space. She was patient and never made me feel inept when I made a mistake. I quickly became one of the top earning stylists. In just over a year, I was the top retail seller in the salon, even outselling her. Despite all of this, my time there would be limited to three years.

Bosses Shouldn't Equal Best Friends

Amidst all the learning behind the chair, a friendship blossomed. I wasn't in a great space mentally or emotionally, and neither was my boss. I was floundering in life. She was going through an ugly divorce. We bonded over our mutual insomnia. In the middle of the night we got together and played pranks on our other coworkers. It was hilarious. We both needed the camaraderie. As much as we helped each other, we also enabled one another. In my solitude of being in a new city with no friends, I lost track of who I was. She was this larger than life person who seemed so awesome and cool. I overlooked the questionable nature of our relationship and decided that no matter what, I was going to be her person. Our friendship made me feel relevant. I wish I could go back and take my own hand and say, "Hey Ron, you're so amazing and relevant all on your own." Because I was. But, I needed somewhere to belong, and she invited me in. We were together constantly. We traveled together, we spent holidays together, her home became my second home. With her, I could avoid focusing on myself.

In the meantime, my coworkers were shitty, and why wouldn't they be? I was a part of the "inner circle." I was under the bosses wing, and they weren't. I was distanced from them for a long time because of it. While they were mad at me for being her person, I was upset with my inability to be in their inner circle. I couldn't have it both ways. If I had it to do over, I don't know that I would've gotten as close to my boss as I did. But, I learned more about myself in those three years than many prior. However, I'm hoping that when you read of how it went up in flames, you won't make the same mistake.

5 Reasons Why NOT to Befriend Your Boss:

1. Favoritism. As much as you might think it's going to excel your career to be buddy-buddy with the boss lady (or man), it won't. It will only create a grey area as large as the Grand Canyon.

2. You run the risk of being asked to do something business related in the name of friendship. It's a great way to end up being manipulated into doing more than your fair share.

3. Anything you do wrong at work might be taken personally. That means, if you slip up, you'll probably be hearing about it later on when you go grab dinner and after-work drinks.

4. You will be held to a higher standard than everyone else.

5. When you decide it's time for you to move on, you run the risk of losing the friendship as well.

The lines of our friendship and work relationship were so blurred there was no way to decipher which was which. I always respected her, especially at work. I worked hard. She would say jump, and I'd ask how high. I wasn't perfect, but I tried my damnedest. Over all, It was a flurry of dysfunction and amazingness all wrapped into one deliciously nauseating burrito-as-big-as-your-head. My stress and anxiety levels were maxed.

When I reached the point of leaving, it didn't go well. Over the course of my final year at Salon B, I'd began learning how to love myself. I learned what it meant to take care of myself emotionally, without needing someone else to need me. I hit the ceiling of growth there and I was burnt out. When I told her I wanted to make a change, it went downhill fast. She got aggressive fast. I got defensive. The personal digs started, and the lines had never been so blurry. I had seen her treat former employees better when they were screaming profanities at her. Things got hostile and the only answer I had was to leave. I told her, "for the sake of our friendship, I don't think I can stay." So I didn't. It's been nearly a year since that happened, and we still aren't speaking. It was the first time in our friendship that I needed to do something big for myself, and it was received like a blow to the head.

I have made it a point to stay distanced from my superiors ever since. I strongly encourage you to do the same. A healthy relationship with your boss happens when your personal life stays at home.

A Giant Sigh of Relief

I hadn't planned on leaving Salon B so abruptly, so I certainly didn't have a plan in place for doing so. I scrambled to find a new salon home. I had a lot of dedicated clients waiting to follow me, and for that to happen, they needed to know where I was.

Enter: Salon C. Aah yes, just typing that made me sigh with relief. The owner called me back right away. We chatted, met the next day, and soon after, they hired me. I was back behind the chair within four days.

Salon C gave me a peaceful space to work. They received me without asking a lot of questions. They were understanding, withheld judgement and opened their arms to me. In no time, I was up and running. The owners of Salon C are brilliant business people. 30 years of operation speaks to their ability to change and evolve with the industry. At Salon C, there was nothing but evolution, opportunities and room to grow.

The owners got into this business to offer people a place to run their businesses without drama. One of the requirements in the handbook is to, "be a little weird." I knew I was in the right place when I read that. They gave performance reviews monthly. As Millennials, that's exactly what we're looking for. When we sit down with our bosses and set goals, it gives us something to strive for. We don't want to be dictated to. We want to be coached. We want to be heard.

We want our ideas to matter. We want to be recognized for our efforts and contributions. That is exactly what I found at Salon C.

Not only did they allow me to switch to a part-time schedule, but they let me pick the days and hours that suited me and my clientele. They didn't shut me out, or get mad. They realized that in order for me to stay, that is what I needed. They didn't take opportunities away from me, or treat me like a lesser member of the team. They gave me the greatest gift, by allowing me the space I needed to be a writer. They cheered me on and lifted me up. They encouraged my ideas and suggestions. That is what a boss/employee relationship is all about! I've never felt so in control of my life while working for someone else. As Millennials, is that not what we're seeking?

We want to live life on our own terms. We want to be given the freedom to be contributing members of the team. We want to be valued. But in order for that to happen, there are some first-world behaviors we need to check in on.

Put Your Best Face Forward.... Hold the Drunken Insta-Posts

Entering the workforce nowadays is hard. There are fewer jobs and stiffer requirements. Starting salaries are low, living expenses are high and job security is nonexistent. If you don't know what you're looking for when you start job hunting, you're going to get chewed up and spit back out. Self-motivated, driven individuals get the best positions. What are you? With so many people battling for jobs, it's crucial that you make yourself marketable. Earlier, I mentioned looking up your future coworkers on social media. What would I find if I looked you up on social media?

It doesn't matter how private you think you've made all your social media accounts, they're never as private as you think they are.

Social Media & The Job Hunt 101:

1. Posting photos of all your drunken escapades may have been fun early on, but it looks bad to a potential employer.

2. 300 of your best posed selfies looks narcissistic and frankly, it's boring. I know you have hobbies. Try having someone else photograph you doing them now and then. Look at me, I'm at the park! On vacation! Running a Marathon! Anything to make you look more interesting. Selfie-addicts are boring.

3. What content are you sharing? Everyone loves funny videos of kittens and babies, they're funny and relatable. But, how many trashy reality show posts are littering your wall? Or foul memes with colorful language? What about fake news? It's helpful if the content you're posting shows you have more depth than your puddle of spilled coffee.

4. What do your Facebook statuses or Tweets say about you? Are they dramatic? Are you constantly using them to complain about your job, family/friends, or life in general? Nobody likes a Victimized Victor. Employers like problem solvers. I don't know about you, but I can't think of the last time someone solved a problem by complaining about it on Twitter.

5. Don't post offensive things. Yes, we all have the right to take a stance on something we believe in, but use caution. Posting an offensive joke or comment can come back to haunt you. I've been known to get into a Facebook debate or two, but I always keep it classy. Attacking people on social media will came back and bite you in the ass sooner or later.

6. Be careful of how often you're posting. If you're posting interesting content several times a day, great. If you're posting useless content 50 times a day, chances are you're not being productive in other aspects of your life. Potential employers will note this.

As a final tip in this section, I beg you to assess your email address. BJohnson@xyz.com is totally acceptable! You could even add an underscore or relevant number at the end if necessary. BJohnsonSeXxyBeastXxOo@YoureATool.com. Need I say more? Sorry SexXy BeastXxOo, no one is going to hire you.

It is encouraged for Millennials to create a strong personal brand via social media. Some industries won't take you seriously without one. Social media allows us to speak publicly about things that older generations didn't, because we have the platform to do it. Scroll down any Facebook feed and you'll see memes, articles, blog posts, speaking to every subject under the sun. The goal? To make people laugh, to bring people together, to start debates, to blow people's minds, etc.

We Are Millennials, Hear Us Roar

There are plenty of people in older generations who consider 20-somethings to be lazy, entitled, narcissistic, unmotivated, disconnected, and disloyal. PHEW, I almost ran out of breath typing that. We know differently. Millennials have a whole slew of awesome qualities to add to the workforce. We just need to make sure our actions are speaking louder than their preconceived notions about us.

> *"One of the primary reasons Millennials are more likely to change jobs is because they are not willing to stick around if they do not believe they are receiving any personal benefit or growth."*
> -Jeff Fromm, forbes.com article on Millennials in the workplace

And why should we? We won't tolerate putting in long hours to stay on the same level. We want to learn, and grow. We will absorb everything you teach us, but if you don't have anywhere for us to grow, we will take what we've learned and implement it elsewhere. This is exactly what happened to me at Salon B. I absorbed everything I was given like a sponge, but then I topped out. What was I supposed to do? Stick around stagnantly out of loyalty? Why would anyone want that? If the heads of companies want Millennials loyalty, they should never run out of productive ways to challenge us.

We aren't lazy, we are just motivated differently. If a project is going to take us eight hours, we will buckle down and spend eight hours on it. If a project that could take less time is made to take longer, we will find a way to do it in less time. Why would we allow ourself to be stuck working unnecessary hours when we could be out adventuring?

We are a wicked innovative generation. We are the generation of Facebook, Uber, start-up companies and living life on our own terms! They say we were too coddled with our, "participation ribbons." Well, I say we know how to value everyone on the team, and get shit done together. Historically as generations age, they become more resistant to change. They pass judgements about younger generations simply because they're pushing for change. They are presenting ideas to overhaul archaic practices and make things more efficient. There has yet to be a generation that doesn't criticize the generation after them. If everyone would embrace the newness, the evolution of old and young working together could be a beautiful thing! According the the pew research center, Millennials are 54 million strong and make up one third of the work force. We are the largest living generation! We have the power to do incredible things, and we're doing them.

Job Hunt Check List

When you're first starting out, it can be difficult to know just what to look for. I've compiled a short list of things to look for when you're doing recon for a job.

1. Is there schedule flexibility?
    - If you're done with a project, are you required to sit around the remainder of the day and twiddle your thumbs?
    - What kind of vacation time is available?

2. Meaningful work relationships
    - Will you have a mentor?
    - Will you have the opportunity to mentor others as you advance?

3. Choices of projects and learning opportunities
    - Are you able to work on projects that highlight your strengths and help you advance?
    - Are advanced learning opportunities available? Does the company pay for them?

4. Advancement opportunities
   - What are the requirements for advances and raises?
   - Are these opportunities merit based or "time-served" based?

5. Will I be able to make a difference here?
   - Is the environment one where every employee has a voice?
   - If you spot an opportunity for improvement and provide a solution, will you be allowed the space to take action?

6. What is covered in the meetings?
   - Are meetings about relevant things, or are they constantly covering the same issues and not rendering results?
   - Do you feel armed with the information you need to go forth and continue your bad-assery, or are you left feeling annoyed and unmotivated?

7. How progressive is the company?
   - When is the last time they rebranded?
   - Is the atmosphere one of progress and change, or do you feel like you just walked into an 80s-era boardroom?

There's no time to waste in a dead-end job. Keep your eyes open, and be present at all times.

Remember these things:

- Set goals or someone else will set them for you.

- You don't owe anyone anything; remember this when you're feeling a false sense of loyalty to someone who isn't helping you progress.

- Personal and professional should be separate. If you think you have to be repeatedly shut down, overworked and underpaid in order to climb the ladder, you're digging yourself an early career grave.

- People will treat you how you allow them to treat you. Know your own worth.

I want you to have a lot of confidence, 20-Something, but don't be an asshole. I'm not saying all of these things so that you can go into a new job and act entitled, like you're better than everyone and own the place. Settle down. You're going to have to work hard for what you want. I just want you to put your energy and solid work ethic into jobs that serve you well. You're going to put a lot of yourself into your career, but be pragmatic about it. Every drop of blood, ounce of sweat and salty tear should be a stepping stone toward your ultimate goals.

Don't give up on something just because it's hard. There's a difference between walking away from a job because you're being taken advantage of, and walking away because you're lazy and just want everything handed to you. Ain't nobody got time for that. You should be working hard. You should have moments when you question your ability, and then you should push yourself even harder. When you're at the right place, going above and beyond what's expected of you can have huge payoffs. You'll be making a brilliant impression and will set yourself up to be the first person your superiors think of when opportunities for growth arise.

Hear me on this point: If you don't decide right now that you're not going to be taken advantage of, you're going to open yourself up to be treated like you're somebody's bitch. Do you want to be somebody's bitch? I didn't think so. Remind yourself every day of your strength and worthiness to be treated equally and with respect. You'll be tested by superiors, male and female; don't let them break you. Check your happiness meter often. If you're moaning and groaning every workday and don't even want to get out of bed, it's time to reevaluate. Don't be a whiny baby. Remember those big girl panties we talked about? Put them on and take control of your life. Make the world your bitch every single day.

Chapter Three
FINDING YOUR HEALTHY

Let me preface this chapter by saying, your weight is only a number on a scale, it doesn't measure your level of intelligence, self-worth, or beauty. This chapter is about being the healthiest version of yourself—physically, mentally and emotionally.

Like millions of 20-something girls, I've had my fair share of body image issues and a pretty unhealthy relationship with food. I used my diet as a control mechanism: When my life felt out of control, I started hyper-focusing on what I could control, like the amount of food I ate. Realistically, this never aided in my losing or gaining weight. I've been within the same 10-pound range since 7th grade.

The truth is, I was fat-phobic. The idea of gaining weight terrified me because my self-worth was completely wrapped up in what size clothes I wore. I spent all of my teens and most of my 20s obsessing over everything I ate. Nothing I did was ever good enough in my eyes. What a horrible waste of time that was.

I won't use this chapter to bombard you with all the reasons why it's useless to lose yourself to the throes of an eating disorder or give you a laundry list of all the ways the media sets impossible standards for what women "should" look like. Eating disorders are a beast. I've seen them completely snuff the light out of people I love. It is a mental illness that needs to be treated with the same care as any other. If you or someone you love are struggling, reach out and find help. Don't try to fight it alone.

That being said, the media is a big ugly bastard; we all know this. I think we can agree that every woman has a different body type and shape. "Healthy" and "thin" are relative terms. They mean something different to everyone and look different from body to body. We are beautiful because we are different, but somehow we still manage to beat ourselves to a pulp over not being skinny enough. How about we stop worrying so much about being skinny and focus on being healthy? What if we stop focusing on aesthetic altogether and realize having a beach body is as simple as having a body and putting in on the beach?

I'm what is so lovingly referred to as "thick": wide in the hips, small in the waist. Pants shopping for me is like a comedy act, shaking and wiggling into various cuts of jeans. Boyfriend-fit jeans (which are supposed to be loose fitting) look like skinny jeans on me that happen to be wider at the ankle. No matter how cute I think they are, they were not created for us thicker-thighed ladies. Sure, I could be all emo about it and decide it means I'm fat (and I've had my moments), or I can stick to what I know, which is that skinny jeans with stretch are where it's at. I don't feel like a goddess in boyfriend fit jeans, so I stopped trying to make it happen.

Not every trend that emerges is going to be a good idea for all of us. It's okay! Find a style you're comfortable in and rock the shit out of it. Whatever you're wearing, own it. Make it yours. I used to say, "just because they make it in your size doesn't mean you should wear it." I no longer subscribe to that way of thinking. If you feel like a goddess in it, wear it.

Weird, Unhealthy Trends

What is this weird cultural obsession with the thigh gap? I for one, will never have one.

#WhiteGirlProblems.

I don't want a thigh gap. It would look ridiculous on me. Some girls can't help the fact that they have one—it's their body type. The majority of women will never have one, no matter how hard they try. What would you do if you achieved this elusive thigh gap, anyway? Would you find some way to use it for party tricks? Would you emerge through the other side of your gap and suddenly discover enlightenment and true happiness? What if you're sitting on the toilet and you drop your phone? Without your lovely thigh meat, it might be lost forever to toilet slosh! Say it with me: "I am not my thigh gap!"

I'm amazed at all of these social media trends floating around meant to help you measure whether or not you're "thin enough." A quick Google search of, "How do I know if I'm thin," led me to a quiz tastefully named, "Am I Fat?"

For the sake of this book, I thought, let me try this out. My result...

Beautiful

Yeah, you're fat. So what? All that means is that there is more of you to love. You're sick of hearing about diets and feeling pressure to lose weight. You don't have a problem with the way you look, and if it bothers other people, too bad. It's not like they're carrying you out of the room with a crane, right?
Get over it people!

Uhm...what? Okay, they weren't totally wrong; I don't have a problem with the way I look, and I am sick of hearing about diets. But, seriously? None of my answers would indicate me being fat. They would however, indicate being confident. The purpose of this quiz is to say that the only way I could possibly be skinny is if I choose all the "obsessive" answers. For Instance, answering that when out to eat I'd do more than drink water. Since I chose all the answers that pointed to confidence (hello, hot cheesy pizza. You sexy beast you), this must mean I'm overweight. How confusing. The trouble, is that girls are taking these quizzes and using them to define their worth.

#Thinspiration

How often have you seen girls posting photos of skinny models with this hashtag? The worst time for this is during the Victoria Secret "Angels" Fashion Show. Ladies, please. These women's entire lives revolve around staying thin. They have professional trainers, and dietitians. When you have 6-8 hours a day to devote to fitness, and have other people cooking your meals, it's easy to look that way. It's not real life. Don't get me started on the use of cigarettes and drugs to help keep weight down as well. For the sake of young girl's body images everywhere, let's stop glorifying this lifestyle. If you need a hashtag, lets pick #Fitspiration with a photo of female athletes that are (typically) the epitome of healthy and strong.

Bikini Bridges and Other Skinny Nonsense

First it was the thigh gap, now it's the bikini bridge. Please allow for a brief pause while I #facepalm for a moment. There are entire Facebook groups dedicated to the glorification of the gap between a woman's hip bones and her bikini bottoms when she lays down. This started as a hoax and has snowballed into a full on "thinspiration mainstream trend." Not only is this adding to the objectification of women, it's also giving women another reason to compete against and harshly judge one another. Shouldn't we be on the same team by now? Your bikini bridge freaks me out. Keep your business covered. Who knows what might come popping out from that gaping space; monsters, tampon strings, your local right-wing politician? I digress. Whenever you see a new trend emerging to measure you on the skinny-meter, do yourself a favor and x off the page.

2 or 22, Happy Isn't a Number

We have this habit of thinking we'll be happier once we reach a certain weight. It's like we'll magically become more worthy of being women if we wear single-digit pant sizes. Maybe one day you'll reach that single digit, and when you do, you'll realize there's just another perceived flaw waiting there to greet you. There are plenty of women running around wearing a size 4 pant who get winded running up a flight of stairs. Ever heard of "skinny fat"? It's a thing. These are people who eat like bears, never workout, but remain a "healthy" weight. They have low muscle mass and similar diagnostic markers to diabetics. All of this equals unhealthy.

There are also women who are overweight and can run half-marathons faster than me. It's fantastic that they exercise and are able to run. The thing is, it's still unhealthy to carry around too much extra weight, even if you are able to run a race while carrying it.

Some how we need to bridge the gap between these two types of people. Hah, bridge the gap, see what I did there? Everyone is different. Yes, you are still beautiful whether you wear a size 2 or a size 22. Let's just aim to be healthy.

What IS Healthy?

Discovering what healthy means, is how I managed to conquer my dysfunctional relationship with food. I admire the many people and groups I see who cheer themselves on: FAT AND PROUD! Okay, that's great. I'm glad you're able to declare your self-pride, but being fat isn't anything to be proud of. Being skinny isn't anything to be proud of either. We are all women. We come in many shapes, sizes. We're all deserving of self-love and acceptance. Choosing to lead a healthier lifestyle doesn't mean you aren't proud of what you look like and who you are. In fact, choosing to make changes out of a place of self-love is imperative to personal growth.

Just because you're fat doesn't mean you're lazy. Having an unhealthy relationship with food is typically not about food at all. It's just another method of numbing out. Some people use drugs and alcohol. Some people use sex. Hell, even binge watching TV every night is a method of numbing out. None of these are healthy. There isn't truly a healthy way to numb out long term. There's no magic pill to fix all your problems. Identifying what you're running away from is the key to overcoming any of these. Working through your shit and learning how to love yourself is a major key here. Couple that with a consistent exercise routine and a healthy diet and you'll be feeling like a brand new you in no time.

You Are What You Eat

Here is the hard truth: you cannot eat shit on the daily and expect clean teeth and minty breath. Eating crap makes you feel like crap, look like crap and maybe even smell like crap. If you find yourself at a drive-thru window multiple times a week, it's time to do some reevaluating. How is fast food serving your desire for a healthier life? It's not. And dammit, it doesn't even taste good! No, don't argue—that processed load of chemicals, salt and sugar does not taste good. It's not even food! And trust me, I used to eat my fair share of fast-food, too. Repeat after me:

"If I want to feel good, I have to eat real food."
I understand the convenience that quick food offers your busy life. The problem, is that when you decide to constantly eat junk, you're deciding that whatever is keeping you so busy is more important than your health. Listen sister, I'm here to tell you, NOTHING is more important than your health. Without it, the time you'll have to enjoy all of life's greatness, is even more limited than it already is. According to the Center for Disease and Control, heart disease is the number one cause of death among both men and women, as well as across most ethnic lines in the United States. Do you know what two major things can be done to avoid it? Stop eating shit, and start exercising.

I can't help it: when I'm on my way home from the gym early in the morning, and I see an entire drive-thru packed with cars, I become judgey. You're starting your day off with a greasy breakfast sandwich? And you're a grown adult? Do you plan to be dead by lunch? It's cheaper to eat at home. If you're in a hurry, grab a banana and some almond butter. You could even have smoothie ingredients ready to toss in the blender. These other food-like substances are not going to sustain your body. Instead, they're going to make you groggy and muck up your blood cells—and your brain. How are you going to live your best life when you're all mucked up with fake food?

Here are a few tips I have found useful in my journey to be healthier:

1. **Prepare Food Ahead of Time.**
   Meal prepping means you decide at the beginning of your week what you want to eat for dinner that week, buy the stuff and make it ahead of time. I know, it's a miraculous concept. A little forethought goes a long way. It's even easy to make breakfast ahead of time so you can grab it the next day when you're running out the door.

2. **Leftovers**
   Make a big pot of something on Sunday night and eat it for the remainder of the week. If you're like

me, you'll use it for lunch and then make something fresh for dinner. It's super-easy and effective.

3. **Recipes**

    I'm not a fancy chef; I'm a normal person. Recipes are great. In the mood for chicken? Perfect, Google search 'healthy chicken recipes' and right before your eyes a large expanse of options will appear! Go get the ingredients and make magic.

Maybe you suck hardcore at cooking. Good news: there are mass amounts of cooking classes you can take in person or watch online for free. Everyone can cook given a few key tips and tricks. "I can't cook" is a cop out. It means you don't want to cook. But, your health is counting on it!

I cook mostly with olive oil, avocado oil and occasionally coconut oil. I don't use mass amounts of butter or salt and I definitely don't use shortening or lard on the regular. Cooking at home will still clog your arteries if you're cooking with a high amount of trans fats. Aside from that, I don't hold back in the kitchen. Make sure you're eating plenty of fresh fruits and veggies. If you eat meat, it should be the smallest thing on your plate and you don't need to eat it at every meal.

Don't start with, "...but Ronni, I don't like vegetables!" You're a damn adult: get over it. You need vegetables if you want a healthy body, that's all there is to it. I generally roast or broil mine in the oven with a drizzle of olive oil, salt and pepper. Veggies are delicious if you take the time to figure out how you like them (and I don't mean slathered in butter and cheese).

Keep your processed food and drink intake to a minimum. They are filled with sugar and trans fats. Watching your sugar intake is a key component to a healthy body. They add sugar to everything (even things that claim to be "sugar free"). The American Heart Association says women shouldn't consume more than 30 grams of sugar per day. That is seven teaspoons. A 12oz can a Coca-Cola has 39g of sugar. One can of soda and BAM, you've reached and exceeded your sugar maximum for the day. Sugar has been found to be just as addictive as cocaine. I've dealt with my fair share of sugar addiction. Any excess amount in your body is turned into fat. There are also 56 different names for sugar on food labels. Food makers will do anything to confuse you. Learn how to read labels and you'll be able to stick it to the man; they wont fool us with their fancy names!

Going home after work and popping a Healthy Choice in the microwave does not a meal make. When you're at the grocery store, aim to stay out of the frozen foods section. It's one thing if you're grabbing a bag of frozen green beans, it's another thing if you're grabbing a box of hot pockets (I know you're lying if you tell me you actually enjoy those). Side note: have you ever watched the Jim Gaffigan skit about Hot Pockets? Go watch it right now, you can thank me later.

I have a habit of watching what other people grab from the shelves while I'm shopping. I can't help it. You can tell a lot about people based on what's in their grocery cart. I once stood in line and watched the person ahead of me unload a couple dozen frozen meals onto the conveyor belt. She had a frozen meal to cover all hours of the day. Needless to say, this woman wasn't exactly a picture of health. I wanted to take all her items, put them back in her cart and say, "Let me help you out; someone accidentally dropped all this garbage in your cart." Instead, I just stood there, mouth agape, wondering how many people in the world eat like this daily. I was not judging this woman as a human being. I was mourning the fact that she probably didn't know any better, or didn't care enough about herself to learn. A great many people eat this way because no one taught them better.

Most of the bad eating habits we have as adults started in childhood. Maybe your parents never cooked, and when they did it was less like cooking and more like opening a package and popping the contents into a microwave. Maybe you don't have the slightest idea what real food is. Real food to you might mean you opened a can rather than drove to a window. Reality: Neither of those options is real food. It isn't your fault that you grew up not knowing the difference. It is your fault if you continue the trend and don't teach yourself better habits.

To recap, let's remember a few things:

1. Thigh gaps are a mythical unicorn.
2. Whatever you're going to wear, wear it like you mean it.
3. Fast food = early grave.
4. Vegetables are our friend.
5. Frozen meals and fast-food don't count as food.
6. Processed sugar lurks in the shadows; watch your back.
7. You're an adult now, you have to learn to cook.

Now, on to everyone's favorite topic to hate:

Exercise!

Running for My Life

Let's rewind back a bit to when I was working at Salon A and hating my life. Running became my life source. I felt I could handle anything on the days that I ran. I decided my goal would be to run a 10k. It's always good to set a goal. I would get up at 5:30 in the morning to get my run in before work. I spent an hour outside running, before the world got loud; just me, feet hitting the pavement, music flowing through my ears, and the meditative rhythm of my breathing. I would go back and forth between thinking of what the day ahead of me would hold, and not thinking at all; just breathing. The further I ran, the more I felt in control and like I could rise above anything I'd be faced with that day. I pushed myself harder than I ever had and I was becoming mentally, physically, and emotionally stronger with every stride.

One night I was trolling Facebook and I saw someone on my newsfeed had posted about a half marathon she was running in Indianapolis. It was called the Indy Women's Half. Hmmm... 13.1 miles. Dare I? After a whole 10 minutes of thought I clicked the link, paid the fee, and I was officially signed up to run a half marathon in three months. Training for that marathon was my new Italy. It was something I was doing for myself, something to keep my mind focused, something to keep my spirits up.

It was the hottest summer we had in years. Temperatures exceeded 100 degrees for days and days, occasionally breaking into a crisp 90-something. I had to get up at the crack of dawn to run because even by 9am it would be too hot. But alas, I ran.

I continued training after I moved to Indianapolis and started working at Salon B. I didn't know anyone, so running was my companion. It was the one familiar thing I had in my new surroundings. One more month passed and finally it was time for the race.

I'd never run a race of any length, so I wasn't exactly sure what to expect, but it was a blast. I pushed myself hard. I could never tell how far ahead or behind the crowd I was. I just kept running, even when I felt like I was going to die. I ended up finishing in 2 hours 28 minutes. I placed in the top half of the runners. I was incredibly proud of myself, a feeling I wasn't all too familiar with back then.

I could lie and tell you I kept running even after that race day, but for a long time, I didn't. My once-constant companion became more of an acquaintance. I ran sporadically, and never for more than a few miles. It just didn't do it for me anymore; it became more of an obligation. For the next couple years my workouts consisted mostly of three-mile jaunts on the treadmill and ab workouts. On top of that, my diet went from healthy to mediocre. I shake my head just thinking about it. Sporadic exercising on top of an unwholesome diet is about as useful as a vibrator with no batteries. Luckily, fitness and I eventually became companions again.

Drop It Like a Squat

You may be an avid gym dweller, or maybe you haven't had any exercise since high school gym class more intense than picking up this book. Whatever your reality, by the time I'm through with you, you'll be frolicking happily to the gym like Julie Andrews through Austrian hills in The Sound Of Music. Okay, maybe you won't. But with any luck, you'll at least put down the soda and go for a walk.

First, I'd like to address the girl we all know and judge: the cardio junkie. We've all seen her, and some of us have been her; she's the girl bobbing along on the treadmill for what seems like an eternity and just when you think she must be done, she leaps off and hits the elliptical for another 40 minutes.

#EyeRoll

This is entirely unnecessary. If you are that girl, stop being that girl: everyone's judging you. Yes, getting your heart rate up multiple times a week for 20 minutes or longer is important. It helps strengthen your heart and keeps your weight down. However, if spending hours on the treadmill, elliptical or whatever other piece of hellacious cardio equipment is your obsession, it isn't doing you any other favors. Cardio won't strengthen your muscles and give you the shape and tone of a healthy body.

My biggest pet peeve is when women get all whiney about weightlifting because they "don't want to get bulky." In order to get bulky you have to try to get bulky. This means taking a ton of different supplements, eating a crazy high-protein diet and lifting heavy weights. You're NOT going to get bulky from casual weightlifting. What you are going to do is turn your body into a calorie-burning machine.

Lifting causes you to burn more calories throughout the day than cardio alone. As your body builds more muscle it's going to become easier for you to burn fat; that's just how it works. Little by little you'll start to see tone in places you've never seen it, especially if you're used to being a cardio junkie. You're going to feel strong and like the total badass that you are. It's so empowering to be able to lift heavy things by yourself without getting winded. As if these benefits aren't awesome enough, you're also going to have more confidence and way more mental clarity.

Here's a rough idea of what my weekly workout schedule looks like:

M	T	W	T	F	S	S
Rest	20 Min Cardio	*Rest*	*Rest*	35 Min Cardio	10 Min Cardio	30 Min Cardio
	40 Min Weight Training			30 Min Weight Training	50 Min Weight Training	30 Min Weight Training

This regimen varies, depending on my schedule. I ride my bike to and from work every day. I also aim to take a few long bike rides for leisure throughout the week. Sometime I run outside for 60+ minutes. The important thing is to have a plan, and stick to it as much as possible. The idea is doing something more active than sitting around spooning Nutella into your mouth...although there is certainly a time and place for that, too. I'm no personal trainer, I just aim to stay active. I'm sure there is room for improvement, but this type of schedule works for me.

Weight Lifting to the Rescue

During my time at Salon B, my mental health was deteriorating. I got very lackadaisical about what I ate, and I worked out here and there, but nothing consistent. In addition to that, I was putting all my energy into building questionably healthy relationships. Not surprisingly, I was having anxiety attacks frequently and suffering from long, dark bouts of depression that I was eventually medicated for.

When I was 27 and had been working at Salon B for almost three years, I decided to start working with a personal trainer, Tess. It was one of the best decisions I've ever made regarding my health. I'm a bit of an overachiever, so my gym visits used to last for hours, resulting in my never being consistent with my workouts. I learned several key weightlifting exercises from Tess, and most importantly, how to perform them with correct form so I wouldn't hurt myself. I learned how a 30-40 minute workout three times per week could completely change my body, and my mind. It took only six months of working out with her before I was able to kick my depression and anxiety meds to the curb. Exercise is a phenomenal antidepressant. I've since stopped sessions with Tess, and now I do my workouts solo. I focus on one or two body parts each workout, and I rarely spend longer than an hour at the gym.

I'm finally in a place with my body that I feel is comfortable for me, and I've never been in as good of shape as I am now—not even when I was training for my marathon. No, I don't have 6-pack abs; yes, I have cellulite on my thighs; no, I don't dwell on these silly details; and I never step on a scale. Sure, it would be cool to have rock-hard abs, but truth be told, I really enjoy eating pizza, and as any trainer will tell you, abs are made in the kitchen, not the gym. As for my cellulite? Even fitness models have it; don't let Photoshop fool you. My happiness level isn't going to increase once I've somehow managed to rid my legs of cellulite or gained that impressive 6-pack. I exercise 3-5 days per week, and I eat healthily 80 percent of the time. I enjoy taking care of my body. It makes me feel good and it keeps my mind clear.

Through a lot of self-discovery and determination, I've found that the more I learned to love myself unconditionally, the happier I became. Working out showed me how much mental strength I have. I love who I am. I love who I see when I look in the mirror, cellulite and all. I'm not waiting around for something to change so I can be happy. I've got the formula, and now you do, too: Self Love + Healthy Eating + Exercise Routine = Success. A healthy lifestyle is my antidepressant.

Dear Self, You're Pretty Damn Awesome

Tell me, how often do you look in the mirror and think, Hey girl, you're so fucking amazing and beautiful. Thank you for everything you accomplished today, and thank you for that bomb ass pizza we had for dinner. Much of the time it's probably more like, Hey girl, you've got another zit on your face, and your eyebrows are uneven. What did you even do today? Don't forget to think about the 20 things you didn't get done. Seriously, pizza for dinner again? You're such a slob. You better get to the gym first thing in the morning. You tell yourself tomorrow you'll do better, and if you don't, you beat yourself up more.

We're in this hideous cycle of punishment and reward with ourselves, and it's got to stop. I don't know about you, but I judge myself way more harshly than I judge other people. If someone else sets out to do something and fails, I don't think any less of them as a human being. If I set out to do something and fail, no matter how big or small, I beat myself up about it. I tell myself over and over that I need to change something about myself in order to be happier or worthy of good things.

It's human nature to want to evolve and improve ourselves. The difference between success and failure is the 'why' behind the change. These days, when I'm about to embark on a new journey or take on a new hobby, I ask myself, why? If the reason is because I think it'll make me more attractive or more likable, I automatically stop myself from doing it until I change my reasoning. Doing something out of self-love is different than doing something out of self-judgment. When I'm able to love myself unconditionally, I can do anything I want. I can reinvent myself as often as I wish because I know I'm doing it from a positive place. I love myself so I'm going to do yoga more often because it makes me feel good. If I miss a week, or a month, I'm not mad at myself; I just accept it and if I want to keep doing yoga, I go back to class again. No harm no foul. Learning to love myself exactly as I am in this very moment is an imperfect practice, but the more vigilant I am about it, the better I get.

It's the same with accepting my emotions. I used to get mad at myself for feeling anything but happy. I'd get irritated at myself if I felt embarrassed or hurt by others. I'd especially get mad at myself if I couldn't articulate why I was angry or upset. I would always feel so stupid for feeling that way. No one gets to make you feel stupid for having feelings—not even yourself. Accept your feelings, and allow yourself to work through them without judgment. Who cares if someone else has different feelings about the situation? They're YOUR feelings, not theirs! No one else can experience life from your point of view, so don't let anyone else dictate your emotions.

Don't compare your chapter 10 to someone else's chapter 15. You're on your own unique and imperfect journey. It's a beautiful thing! Be healthy, forgive yourself for whatever it is you keep beating yourself up about, and get out there and kick some ass.

Chapter Four
LOVE:
IT'S OVERRATED TILL IT'S NOT

---

*"We're all a little weird.
And life is a little weird.
And when we find someone whose weirdness is compatible with ours, we join up with them and fall into mutually satisfying weirdness—and call it love—true love."*

- Robert Fulghum

Have you been looking for love in all the wrong places? Maybe all this talk of finding the elusive "one," and falling for them madly and deeply has you giving a heavy sigh and a hard eye roll. That was my reaction for a long time; until I realized the truth; love is completely overrated... until it's not.

Love Yourself First

Having the ability to love starts with loving yourself. You can't truly love another person without conditions and boundaries, until you care for yourself that way. I know hearing this can be aggravating and feel cliché, but it is what it is. Be the love you want to receive, and your life will be fulfilled regardless of whether or not you ever find "the one." Here's how to start loving yourself:

6 Steps to Loving Yourself

1. **Be Decisive.**
   Connect with your deepest needs and desires. Get in touch with all those ooey-gooey feelings; the ones that freak you out and make you want to run and hide. Dive deep into your vulnerability and decide who you want to be and what you want out of life.

2. **Get Honest.**
   What are your inner struggles? Whatever you struggle with, say it out loud, admit it, own it, and then squash it. This won't happen overnight, but until you really face your demons head on, you'll keep making the same mistakes over and over. If you seem to keep picking the same douche-bag partners, dig deep and ask yourself why. Chances are, you're compensating for something you think you lack. Let's get real and move forward!

3. **Accept What Is.**
We've all been hurt in the past. Some of us more than others. We've all made tons of mistakes. Rather than spending time wishing you had done something different, or wishing things had panned out differently, accept that they didn't. You cannot go back and undo shit. You could continue to let those discretions haunt you and control how you function; or you can unload that heaviness. Too many times we use this stuff to define us, or excuse our behavior. "I can never trust anyone again because I was cheated on. It is what it is." Girl, no, this is not how it is; this is how you're making it. You are not a victim. You get to decide what controls your life, and what story you tell yourself. Carrying around bitterness, resentment and hate isn't about the other person, it's about you. You get to forgive because it's healthy for you, it's not about the other person. Acknowledge what hurt, process through it, forgive and move on.

4. **Lose Judgement.**
Accept who you are right now. This might be the most important factor in being able to love unconditionally. Everybody who doesn't fully love themselves thinks, "I'll be happy when..." You fill in the blank for yourself. Maybe it's when you lose weight, or gain that good old bikini bridge. Maybe it's when your bank account is fatter or when you can afford to vacation every three months. The trouble is, you're constantly trying to reach for these things, and until you conquer them, you always see yourself as less than. When you can accept yourself no matter what, it's easy to set goals and reach them, because you're doing it out of love for yourself rather than judgement. It's way more pleasant. I don't know about you, but I am much more likely to succeed when I act out of love instead of judgement.

5. **Head North.**
   Figure out what career, hobbies and type of people inspire you and make you feel all giddy and excited. Make sure your life reflects those things. Follow your true north.

6. **Stop Complaining and Gossiping.**
   Of course, we're all going to have our moments. "What is she wearing right now? Are those even pants," you scoff, as you take a bite of your blueberry scone. It's fine, we're all human. However, if you're always complaining and gossiping is perpetuate more unpleasantness. That's some low vibrational shit. Happy people don't align themselves with negativity.

Loving yourself isn't a perfect practice, but all the hard work is worth it. The sooner you're able to embrace yourself, the happier you'll be.

Love Is...Love Isn't

Love is a choice. It's a mess of emotions, as tangled as last years Christmas lights. It's a place where you can completely embrace each other's quirks and weirdness, (the way you fart and then look around like you're not sure where it came from is so cute, babe). It is forgiving, open and honest. True love is unconditional, and worth the effort.

Love isn't a disney fairytale. It's not a tidy little package filled with hearts and butterflies. There's no room for judgement or self-consciousness, for pointing fingers or placing blame. It's not keeping secrets or feeling the need to stifle your true self.

How to Know You've Met the Right One

- You miss them when you're apart.
- You want your family and friends to like them.

- You get excited about their ccomplishments (even if yours are a little stagnant lately).

- You want to do things for them just to see them smile.

- Your sense of self has grown by being with them.

- You enjoy participating in each other's interests and hobbies.

- You communicate openly about your thoughts and feelings.

- You aren't freaked out by committing to them.

The Art of Modern Dating

Finding love online isn't just common, it's a brilliant modern ritual. It doesn't carry the same stigma that it did ten years ago. You're not a failure or a loser for meeting your lover on the internet. We live hectic lives. If you didn't meet your honey in college, you don't work with anyone of interest, and your friends are useless at hooking you up...online dating might be exactly what you need.

Use multiple dating sites, depending on what you're looking for. eHarmony and Match tend to offer a slightly more serious and mature crowd and emphasize long-lasting relationships. They also cost $$. My favorite free sites are OkCupid and Tinder. I don't care what anyone says, Tinder isn't just a hookup site. Sure, some people use it that way; but, I know quite a few people who have found long lasting love in the Tindersphere (Even I became someone's Tinderella). There are also a ton of specialized sites out there. There is one for just about anyone; various religious organizations, single parents, farmers, gold diggers...you name it!

It's helpful to have an idea of what you will and won't tolerate before embarking on any dating expedition. Setting boundaries is important, and knowing what your deal breakers are is imperative.

Online Dating Do's

DO add an array of photos that show you doing many different things. Include at least one full body shot (preferably clothed) (wink!), and make sure you show yourself doing activities you enjoy (travel photos are great!). Most importantly, make sure your photos are recent.

DO have a straightforward list of important things about yourself. Be thoughtful, ask yourself if the points you're making are describing uniquely you, or are making you sound basic and describing every modern woman (I love yoga. I love food. I love to laugh and have a good time). Okay, yeah, who doesn't?

DO be careful how much info you give out. No one needs to know where you work.

DO always meet in a public place. This goes for more than just the first date! One date doesn't turn them into a trustworthy person.

DO be aggressive and make the first move. Ladies, it's acceptable and preferable for you to send the first message. Go get 'em you modern vixen.

DO keep an open mind when you go on a first date.

DO have fun and try not to take everything so seriously. These things take time.

& Don'ts

DON'T have more than one selfie.
I'm being generous by even allowing one.

DON'T add group photos.
No one wants to play Where's Waldo.

DON'T give misleading information. They're going to figure it out eventually anyway. Be upfront.

DON'T write a novel. Nobody will read it anyway.

DON'T give your phone number out to every hottie that sends you a message.

DON'T get into cars with strangers.
Basic kindergarten lessons here folks.

DON'T use the first date as a marriage interview. Just go with it.

Pursuing a Love Interest

Let's assume you've made it past the first few amazing (and slightly awkward) dates. If you're still digging the person, the next actions you take ar e important. Here are some tips to make it as successful as possible:

- "I love you" rarely needs to come up before the one-month meet-a-versary.

- Posting all over social media about your new found relationship is a recipe for disaster. You're inviting all your followers to insert themselves into your love-life. The happiest couples I know, rarely post about their love lives online.

- A new relationship is fun, but also sensitive. You're testing the waters, seeing how much you can trust your heart with this person. The more open you are the better.

- Pay attention to what your new mate isn't saying. Actions speak much, much louder than words. If they say they can't wait to see you, but then act flighty when you're trying to make plans, this is a red flag.

- I know label makers are fun, but try to leave them out of the first month or two of your relationship. Don't rush into calling each other boyfriend/girlfriend. Sometimes it's too much pressure for a fragile new "thing."

- Families are great (mostly), but don't feel like you need to rush into introducing each other to your prospective families. When the time comes, don't play the, "you-first-no-you-first," game.

- Don't forget about your friends and other relationships. Don't be that girl. Balance is key.

- Set boundaries and don't be afraid to stick to them. Maybe you don't want to have sex for now; that's perfectly fine. If the other person can't adhere to that, then show them the door.

- Make sure you're on the same page about what the relationship is. If he wants things on "Netflix and Chill" mode and you'd really like to hold hands and make future plans, it's cool to move on.

- Make sure you keep your independence. Don't lose the ability to take care of yourself simply because you're falling in love.

* **Netflix and Chill:**
(verb) A code for having sex.

Quirky Rituals = Healthy Couples

One of the best parts about being in a relationship are the cute, weird little things you do that make you both laugh, and keep things light. They are seemingly meaningless little actions that you bond deeply over. Here are a few quirky rituals as told by a some anonymous contributors.

———————

"We walk up behind each other and give each other wedgies while simultaneously saying, 'brown line!' and then laugh hysterically as the other person digs their underwear out of their butt."

- *Jane*, 28

"We don't seem capable of getting through an entire show without pausing it a million times to talk about something that's happening. We always sit down with the best intentions of having an "epic Netflix binge," but only ever make it through one or two episode...in five hours."

- *Julie*, 26

"When we first moved in together he insisted we not be shy to poop in front of each other. I was hesitant. One morning he came into the bathroom while I was on the toilet. I said, "You better walk back out, its about to get real in here." He said, "Just poop, its fine." I said firmly, "No! It's going to be a bad one!" Enthusiastically he said, "JUST GO! JUST DO IT!" I yelled back, "OMG! IT'S SO BAD!" But, I couldn't hold it anymore. After that, pooping in front of each other was the most natural thing in the world. That's intimacy, folks."

— *Kate*, 27

"I have chronic constipation, and whenever I have a really successful poop, I run out of the bathroom, declare my success, and we both yell and cheer like it's the greatest victory ever."

— *Rowan*, 25

"We end every day by each giving one reason why we love each other."

— *Gwen*, 29

"He pretends he's eating my face because he loves the way my skin feels and smells. It's a daily ritual."

— *Jasmine*, 30

"When we first started dating we took the 5 Love Languages quiz by Dr. Gary Chapman. My boyfriend was reading his results and his number one was physical touch. I looked over at him seriously, and without blinking or breaking eye contact, I slowly reached out and laid my pointer finger on his forearm. We both cracked up and a ritual was born. Some couples hold hands, we lay pointer fingers."

— *Jackie*, 28

"From time to time while we're cuddling, I'll start rubbing my face on my man's 5 o'clock shadow while simultaneously trying to bite the little hairs which make a funny crunching sound. We both crack up every time; it's like a dog grooming it's partner."

— *Fae*, 27

"One time we were cracking up about something and my teeth got dry. My upper lip got stuck on them, causing us to crack up even harder. Now one of us will purposely rub our upper teeth dry and push our lip up so it gets stuck. The other person will follow suit and we both fall out laughing; it never gets old."

— *Sam*, 29

"When we're walking, we have a game we play where we try to swing our hands together without looking and yell, "magnets!" We do this until we manage to lock our fingers together perfectly. When we succeed on the first try, we both get really excited and high five."

Should I Stay or Should I Go?

Arguably, one of the hardest decisions you'll ever have to make is whether or not to stay in a relationship. Love blurs the lines of logic, making it nearly impossible to see the right answer sometimes. Lucky for you, I've made you a checklist.

When to Let Go: ✓
The Checklist

☐ 1. You've realized you don't fully trust them.

☐ 2. Your closest friends and family are voicing concern.

☐ 3. You've tried and failed numerous times to reignite the spark you once had.

☐ 4. You find you disagree on important aspects of life (perspectives on social issues, parenting, finances, religion, politics, etc).

☐ 5. You repeatedly fight about the same things.

☐ 6. You no longer find their quirks endearing (more like super annoying).

- [ ] 7. You don't feel like you're being yourself anymore.

- [ ] 8. Spending time alone watching Netflix and snuggling your puppy always sounds more fun than hanging with your beau.

- [ ] 9. You've already broken up and gotten back together more than once.

- [ ] 10. The sex is the only positive aspect of your relationship.

- [ ] 11. Your both constantly picking fights with one another.

- [ ] 12. You find yourself frequently wondering what else is out there.

- [ ] 13. You constantly feel like you're not a priority to them.

- [ ] 14. You're waiting for your partner to make a major change in order for things to move forward.

☐ 15. You're reading this list eagerly hoping for permission to dump them.

☐ 16. You find reasons not to spend time with them.

☐ 17. You're crushing hard on someone else.

☐ 18. You can't picture your future with them.

At the end of the day, only you can decide whether or not you're ready to call it quits. But, if you put a check mark next to at least two of those, it might be time to take a hard look at the future of the relationship.

Stay true to yourself 20-something. Don't lose sight of your desires, wants and needs. Love takes time, effort and ultimate honesty. If you find yourself getting frustrated by all the duds you seem to be meeting, take a step back and reevaluate. When you're honoring your wants and needs, and walking in your truth, you're bound to meet the right person along the way. Don't force something that isn't.

Chapter Five
FINDING YOUR LOVE TRIBE

"A Love Tribe is a support group for being human. The point is to form a new family—a community who's willing to cheer you on when you're being brave, lift you up when you're down, and believe in you when you don't believe in yourself."

- Vironika Tugaleva

Being a woman is powerful, but being part of a tribe of women who love you is empowering. Your tribe will sweep you up during your darkest hour and love you when you struggle to love yourself. It's an unstoppable force that will help you survive, and remind you how to be true to yourself amid the chaos and demands of everyday life. It's your life raft when you're in over your head and tired of treading water. The women in your tribe are the loudest ones cheering you on in victory—a gang of spirited supporters campaigning for your victory. Don't underestimate the ability of a group of women coming together for a single cause... and sometimes that cause will be you.

There was a time that women would do everything together: raise their children, cook, and tackle daily chores. They spent every day with one another forming bonds and building each other up. They used to dedicate a place in their village, so cleverly named the "red tent," where during biblical times, women would gather after pregnancy or during menstruation. I imagine this place to be a magical land of unlimited amounts of chocolate and tacos.

A land with muscular, tattooed men massaging their women's backs and feet while they binge-watch Grey's Anatomy, do crafts, and drink wine. Hmmm...this red-tent business sounds like it might be alright.

These days, we are a lot more separated. Our hectic schedules and significant others keep us from being as connected to other women as our ancestors once were. But, that doesn't mean it's any less important to find your support system. We're social creatures who need to be loved and understood. The relationships you have with your tribe will strengthen other relationships in your life. You can't expect your significant other to be everything. If you're relying on your partner for every want and need, you're going to burn him or her out. Remember to cut your mate a break sometimes and find your renewal while hanging out with your friends; it's a must! Don't have a love tribe? I've got ya covered in six easy steps.

6 Steps to Creating Your Tribe:

1. Decide your why. Decide what you want from your tribe, and what kind of people you want to be a part of it. Do you want friends to help you with a new business venture, or maybe girlfriends to go on adventures with? Do you want members who share your spirituality or desire for self-improvement? You may just be tired of feeling alone; that's a great reason to find new friends. Whatever the reason, decide your why, and who, and set your intentions.

2. Know yourself. Be confident in yourself. If you don't know who you are, or who you want to be, you'll struggle to find a tribe. You'll change your opinions and views depending on who you're hanging out with, and it'll be hard to really connect with anyone. Know yourself and what you believe in, and the right people will find their way to you.

3. Stay open-minded. Don't be quick to judge others. Feeling insecure around new people makes you feel vulnerable and causes you to pass quick judgments on people to protect your fragile heart. Embrace the vulnerability. When you're open and authentic, you'll find others who are, too.

4. Look beyond the surface. You might meet someone who seems way too cool to be your friend. Don't be afraid to approach anyone. You might find that you have an immediate connection. Or, you might find out they're shallow and fake, even though they seemed awesome at first. It's okay to cut ties. You can wrap smelly poop in a beautifully decorated box, but there's still just smelly poop inside. Don't be fooled by people who are full of crap, no matter how pretty they are.

5. Reach out. Find or create events in your area that attract people who are like-minded. Whether it's a book club, fitness group, wine club (um, yes please!), or bike gang, seek it out. You can also write blogs on a specific topic or start a social media group and create a virtual tribe.

6. Give compliments. After you've met new people, let them know you enjoyed their company and ask if they want to hang out sometime. If it's individuals who are living the lifestyle you want, let them know how much you respect and admire what they're doing with their lives. A few well-placed, genuine compliments can be effective when you're building new relationships. I know you're excited, but don't over-praise: you don't want to scare them off.

My first tribe was created in high school. We'd all known each other much longer but until we were thrown into the chaos that is ninth grade, we didn't know how much we'd need to pull together to survive. There were five of us, and we called ourselves The Pentagon. Over the next four years, we were each other's lifelines. We spent our summers at the pool or floating down rivers. Winters were for movies and making gingerbread houses. At sleepovers, we stayed up all night talking about life and boys and bingeing on sugar and fast food.

Our sisterhood was like a tiny band of teenaged psychologists. A Pentagon member showing up to school wearing the same outfit twice in a row was a sure sign to be on alert for other concerning behavior (maybe she woke up late, or maybe she was diving into the depths of depression). Beyoncé's "Single Ladies" playing on repeat meant she was feeling happy, free and like the strong, independent woman she was. If someone was home alone watching The Notebook, we knew it was time for an intervention.

We had a lot of major transformations, both individually and together. Newcomers to the group, new relationships, family problems, you name it—it was a rollercoaster of emotions as we tried to keep up with one another. But, those girls kept me honest with myself, and that's exactly what your tribe should do. These days, three of us from The Pentagon are still close. I love them fiercely and I can't begin to list all the ways they've saved me over the years.

I've gained and lost many other friends since the Pentagon days. I know some of my friends will be part of my story forever, and others are only meant to be a chapter or footnote. The key is to know when to hang on and when to let go. Some friendships drift naturally with no hard feelings, and mutual understanding. Other times, people will abruptly become fire-breathing dragons and try to take you down in flames with them. In those instances, it's better to run screaming than to stick around and throw cups of water on a raging inferno.

What I've realized is that your love tribe doesn't have to look a certain way. Chances are, you're going to have different tribes for different reasons. One of my groups is a handful of people who live scattered around the country. I've moved around quite a bit, and so have they. I know if I need any of them, they are just a phone call away. I also have a posse of four or five women of varying ages and backgrounds helping me write this book. Before I started this project, I didn't know any of them; now I have a brand new cheering squad who help keep me on task and encourage me through this labor of love. Another is a Facebook group of over 200,000 women who all love to travel. They keep me inspired and help me keep my eye on the ultimate prize, which for me is to experience the world at large.

Don't hang on too tightly if things start to go awry. Sometimes you need room to grow, and you should never feel guilty for needing space. The people who are meant to stick with you will always come back around. Let the ones go who want to go. Understand that your friends will hurt you, and sometimes you will hurt them. It's not intentional; it's just the way life works. Be gentle with each other. Be forgiving. Make it a priority to see one another, take an annual trip to meet up and reconnect; make an effort. The older you get, the harder it is to maintain friendships, but that doesn't mean you shouldn't try. Put in the time, because when everything falls apart, it's your love tribe that's going to be there to pick you up off the floor and put you back together.

19 Times Your Tribe Will Save the Day

1. When you need help composing the perfect message to a new love interest (Do I start with "Hey!" or should it be like, "Oh hello, you." Too creepy?).

2. When you have your first traumatic home haircolor incident.

3. When you're creating your first online dating profile and don't know how to describe yourself.

4. When you need help figuring out what pop culture phrases mean (She said my eyebrows were "on fleek*," should I be offended ?).

5. When you're in a hurry to get ready and don't have time to shower, your always-prepared friend introduces you to the whore bath (Pits, tits and naughty bits. Carol, get moving!).

6. When you take your first road trip together and realize you've passed the last rest stop for the next 75 miles (Pull the car over and cover me: my bladder won't last that long!).

7. When you lose your virginity and have your first, "oh-my-god-what-if-I'm-pregnant?" freak-out, and need to be taken shopping for your very first home pregnancy test.

8. When you get your heart broken by a total douchebag who wasn't good enough for you anyway (Are we too old to Saran Wrap his car, though?).

9. When you need ice cream and sappy movies after said break-up (It's okay, Carol, if he can't handle your trumpet butt: he was never meant to join the band.).

10. When you get too drunk and need someone to hold your puke bag (It's best if that puke bag doesn't end up splattered all over the sidewalk—not that I've experienced that or anything...).

11. When you're in panic mode about your direction in life (for the thousandth time) and need a reminder of your total badassery.

12. When you drunk-dial each other to declare your undying love for one another. Just in time to save you from wallowing in loneliness when you're out partying with new people who just don't, "get you."

13. When you start to forget how awesome you are and need a reminder.

14. When you get your first "grown-up job," and call them first because you know they will be as excited as you are.

15. When you run out of money and need shaving cream and bagels, and they spot you $10 bucks.

16. When you get the first-day-of-school jitters before your first day at a new job and need some words of needed encouragement.

17. When you both buy the bigger data plan so you can spend more time talking and texting when life takes you thousands of miles away from each other (Help! I don't know how to make new friends anymore! Why did I even move? How did I get here?).

18. When you have a fight with the love of your life and need help dissecting what happened.

19. When it's your wedding day and your (mostly) insane family is making you want to pull your hair out (It's fine, Carol, here's half a Xanax and another mimosa. Everything is going to be great!).

* On Fleek: (adj)
1. A state of flawlessness.
2. A Combination of "fly" and "sleek."

People talk about finding a soulmate in reference to the person one will marry, but I've always thought about soulmates in reference to my friends. Deep connections wear many masks. The majority of the soul-level connections I've made over the course of my life have been with my friends. I learned how to love unconditionally because of my relationships with the people who make up my tribe. I learned how to be my authentic self, for better or worse, without worrying that showing weakness would drive people away. My tribe members have been a part of my journey for varying periods of time, but they each hold a very unique part of my heart.

Chapter Six
CAREER VS. PASSION

"There is no passion to be found playing small—in settling for a life that is less than the one you are capable of living."

- Nelson Mandela

What do you want to be when you grow up? If you're like me, you've had to answer this more times than you can count. From the age of three until I was old enough to start doubting myself, I told everyone I was going to be a famous singer. Over the years this goal began to shift. In the sixth grade I was going to be a WNBA-playing famous singer. What can I say, I've always had lofty goals.

The trouble is, I grew into my self-doubt. Without having anyone around me who had gone the "starving artist" route, I had no idea what to do to follow my dreams. I rarely entertained the thought of doing anything other than singing; I lived and breathed music. The closer I got to high school graduation, the more panicked I became. What the hell was I going to do with the rest of my life? I had to do something. Heaven forbid I would become one of those people who never leave their hometown and become boring.

Many of the people I interviewed for this book chose their major in college based on what came easily to them. Their thinking was, "Math and science are effortless for me, so I'll study engineering," or something similar. Here's the thing: just because something takes little effort for you to perform well, doesn't mean you'll be happy making it into a career. One of my favorite life and success coaches, Danielle LaPorte, says, "Be careful what you're good at, you might end up doing it the rest of your life." PREACH, GIRL, PREACH!

When I asked people if they loved their jobs, many said things like, "Love is a very strong word," or "Sure, I mean, I like what I do." There was a lot of hesitation. Some even registered a slight expression of confusion, as though they had never stopped to consider how much they enjoy their career choices. Why does the idea that we should love what we do seem so outlandish?

Think about what you do to make money every day. Do you love it? Does it fill you to the brim with joy and light you up? Can you get so absorbed in it you lose all track of time? When you're tired from a long day of doing whatever it is you do, are you still excited? Do you believe it's possible to find such a thing?

When I chose to become a hairstylist, I didn't know if I'd be good at it, let alone love it. Knowing myself and my artistic abilities, I decided to give it a go. As it turned out, I was good at it, and I enjoyed it. Early in my career I loved styling hair and doing makeup. Those were the two things that brought me the most joy. I was having a blast. I had dreams of working backstage at Fashion Week in New York, LA, Milan, and Paris. Unfortunately, that's not how things turned out. Looking back, I realize that self-doubt and fear kept me from pursuing my passion. I wouldve had to move to New York City or LA and work under artists who were already doing what I wanted to do—artists who would rip me apart before they could build me up. I knew it would be scary. I would've needed to channel a level of bravery I wasn't sure I had. At the age of 21, I didn't feel ready to jump.

Instead, I went another route. Fast-forward to today: I've spent time being an educator, and I've spent five years behind the stylist chair. I enjoy what I do; I get to hang out with awesome people every day while we all make money doing the hair of interesting clients. Maybe this wasn't the intended route, but it has been a hell of a ride. Sometimes detours are necessary in order for us land exactly where we are supposed to be. For me, every step I've taken and decision I've made has led me to writing this book.

My motivation behind the chair had been waning for quite some time. When my intuition nudged me to cut my hours down to part-time, I took her advice. Just like that, my mood and enthusiasm (and frankly, my hustle) was back. I'm more driven than I have been in years. I remembered why I love doing hair so much. Now, I had the space to figure out what I was missing and what to do about it. The opportunity to write this book all but fell in my lap. It took almost no time for me to remember how much fulfillment I've always gotten from writing.

Sometimes you have to do what seems scary in order to put yourself on the path to finding your true north. If I hadn't created the space in my schedule, I might've missed the opportunity to pursue this new writing path. Sure, I'm going to take a bit of a pay cut for a while, but c'est la vie. I'd rather that than lose my soul to stagnation for the sake of a paycheck. I've put myself in a position to follow both of my passions at the same time.

7 Ways to Know You've Found Your Passion:

1. The idea of it stirs up a fire in your belly.
2. You recognize it like an old friend. It makes you feel warm and fuzzy.
3. You have no regard for time when you're doing it.
4. You want to scream from the rooftops about it.
5. You immediately start making lists of all the things you need to do to accomplish it.
6. That list doesn't feel overwhelming; it feels exciting.
7. The idea of not following that dream leaves you feeling listless and depressed.

When was the last time you followed a path that scared the hell out of you? I knew I'd made the right decision to write professionally because I was terrified in the best possible way. You have to force yourself out of your comfort zone. Greatness happens when growth happens, and growth doesn't happen when you're comfortable.

What Does It Take to Build on Your Passion? It takes:

- Having purpose and drive.
- Summoning grit and determination.
- Removing "what ifs" and "failure" from your vocabulary.
- Throwing your back-up plan out the window, because you'll do whatever it takes to make a reality.
- Trusting in yourself.
- Staying connected to your "why."

What Does Working in a Job Feel Like?

- Obligatory
- Monotonous
- You'd rather poke your eyes out than do it for one more day.
- Paying your dues.
- Stagnant
- Yawn-inducing

When you're working toward your passion, it feels different than working for a job. You will still have to work hard, and some days will be more difficult than others, but you'll be working with a purpose. Your purpose! Building your own dream makes the hard work worth it. Working passionately will never feel monotonous. I have days when I don't feel like writing, but the days I feel excited and motivated way out-number those days. When I'm not feeling creative, I work on some other aspect of my writing career instead, like revamping my website, reaching out to new contacts, or searching for new writing opportunities. You could be doing something every day to push yourself closer to your dreams.

If you haven't found your passion yet, don't panic. Everyone finds theirs in their own time. Your goal should be to stay vigilant. Pay attention to how often you'd describe your feelings in a positive way. You know that gut-wrenching agony you feel after you've finally wrestled all fifteen bags of groceries up the stairs to your apartment, only to realize you left your keys on the front seat of your car? If going to work every day makes you feel like this, it might be time to move on. You might change career paths six times before you find your passion, and that's okay! The important thing is that you put yourself on a path to figuring it out.

Your brilliance and uniqueness are already inside of you. They can stay silent for years before something comes along and causes the spark that will grow into a full-blown inferno of passion. Somewhere along the line a new friend, love interest, teacher, event or opportunity might come into your life, and then, with very little warning, you have your big "aha!" moment. You know what your life's work is going to be about. When it happens, drop everything and listen. Think of yourself as a host. A brilliant idea might find its way to you. If you choose not to pursue it, it will leave you and find someone more willing to bring it to life. Ideas are floating around all the time, waiting to find the right person to turn them into a reality. If you won't do it, someone else will.

We Millennials and Gen Z-ers, as a whole, are determined to follow our passions. It's what drives us. It's what makes us great. We are prepared to have multiple careers, and do whatever it takes to live our dreams. We are constantly seeking ways to work smarter, not harder. We want to travel and explore. We want exciting lives that vary day to day, which is significantly different from what our parents' and grandparents' dreams were.

Most of us grew up with parents who focused on one career. My parents worked for corporate America. I frequently listened to them discuss the ups and downs of their jobs. It convinced me of one thing: I would never—not a day in my life—work in a cubicle. For many of our parents, the top priority was that our families had security. Having money to buy a house, car, and health insurance was where they placed importance. How could we expect them to know how to push us toward our passions rather than just a career? Many of us have to do this for ourselves. We are forging our own paths, 20-Something. Are you excited yet?

What Is Your Why?

Cynics (especially those who are money driven) will scoff at the idea of pursuing something because of the joy it brings. Not everyone's passions will be lucrative. That's not to say you can't make money doing them, but if money is your driving force, then chances are you're going to go after something that supports your desire to make millions. Money isn't my why (though it's incredibly helpful). The driving force for me is freedom. I don't want to be forced to function on someone else's schedule. I want the freedom to take my work with me anywhere I go, and travel the world. It isn't just some pipe dream, it's the path I have put myself on. I've changed my day-to-day routine in order to start living by the standards of my dreams.

What is your why? If you hate going to work every day, do something about it. Allow yourself the space to discover the dream that intoxicates you. That's what being in your 20s is all about. Don't waste this precious time doing things you hate, and working jobs that make you want to pull your hair out. Don't sit through another tedious meeting, listening to people talk at you like a Charlie Brown schoolteacher. Instead, break down the walls of that cubicle, burn that time card and decide right now you're not going to waste another day. Find your purpose, then live and breathe it.

So 20-Something, now is your time. Don't wait around for someone to give you the answers or hold your hand and show you how to find your bliss. Don't be afraid to follow uncommon paths in order to live the life you love. Make sure you're doing at least one thing every day that lights you up and pushes you toward experiencing your most passionate life. It won't always look fiery and unstoppable. Some days, it looks like the steady grind of hard work that is teaching you what you need in order to guide you to the next step. Finding your passion doesn't mean you get to coast: it gives your actions a purpose.

Live purposefully, by your own rules. Trust yourself to know what's best for you and power on!

Chapter Seven
EDUCATION: A BIG GREY AREA

"Education is the movement from darkness to light."
- Allan Bloom

There are two types of higher education: traditional and non-traditional. Traditional education options include associate programs, 4-year colleges, and grad schools. Non-traditional education is everything else...from on-the-job training to online courses and trade schools, to traveling with programs like Americorps or the Peace Corps.

There are plenty of reasons to go the traditional route. If you've known you wanted to be a doctor since you got your first Fisher-Price doctor kit, then you're going to need to go to college. However, if you don't know what you want to be "when you grow up," traditional education may not be for you.

During my senior year of high school, I started panicking about college. All my friends were going, and miraculously, they all seemed to know what they were born to study; and there I was, with no earthly idea what I wanted to do. I knew I was good at singing, but I didn't know how to turn it into a career. I thought teaching music was my only option and I didn't want to teach. I had always been told I was a strong writer, but the idea of pursuing that in college didn't even enter my mind. I had very little direction. No one told me what my other options were if I didn't go to college.

If you're like I was, and you have no idea what sounds fun enough to do for the next six decades, then maybe you should take a year or two off to consider all your options. College isn't for everyone. Many people go to college to find themselves, and for some, that's a great idea; but it's expensive to use college as a means of finding yourself.

We're all made to believe we have to go to college in order to succeed in life. We have to go if we expect anyone who matters to take us seriously. We shell out tens of thousands of dollars, taking out enormous loans and digging our debt holes as early as the age of 18, all in the name of education. We're led to believe if we don't go to college, we'll never get a job, we'll never have money, we'll never amount to anything legitimate. My disdain for the education industry is justifiable: expecting 18-year-olds to know what they want to do with the rest of their lives is insane.

Don't let anyone pressure you into going to college. If it's not for you, it's not for you. Education can be found in every nook and cranny of the world we live in. There are many beautiful and mind-blowing ways to learn.

Taking a non-traditional route may be just what you need. Trade schools and associate programs are a phenomenal way to get the education you want without going into loads of debt. There will likely be some prerequisite classes you'll have to take, but associate programs will have you learning about things directly related to your chosen field in no time. These programs last anywhere from several months to a couple of years. Here are some examples of jobs you can do without going to a four-year college, and their median incomes:

Diagnostic Medical Sonographer..... $68.9k
Choreographer.. $51.5k
Massage Therapist................................ $38k
Computer Support Specialist........... $62.2k
Web Developer..................................... $64.9k
Radiation Therapist............................. $80.2k
MRI Technologist.................................. $67.7k
Medical Assistant................................. $30.5k
Surgical Technologist......................... $43k
Wind Turbine Technician................... $51k
Physical Therapist Assistant.............. $55.1k
Veterinary Technician......................... $31.8k
Dental Hygienist $72.3k
Air Traffic Controller........................... $122.5k

I don't know about you, but some of those median salaries made my jaw drop. When you're looking at that chart, take into consideration that time and experience are going to play a big role in how much you make. You probably won't start off at that salary, but given time, you'll have the opportunity to make even more than those amounts listed. One of the coolest things I found about going with a trade school was that I was already well into my career and making a decent salary before my peers had even finished their undergrad degrees. And, let me tell you, as a cosmetologist, I've been making more than $31k since year two. It's all in how dedicated you are to becoming the best in your craft.

---

http://money.usnews.com/money/careers/slideshow/25-best-jobs-that-dont-require-a-college-degree

http://career-profiles.careertrends.com/stories/22418/highest-paying-jobs-no-college-degree#Intro

Test The Waters: Dip a Toe In

Another awesome idea would be to take some free classes before committing to a college major and regretting it later. There are spectacular resources floating around in cyberspace just waiting for you to discover them.

You can get free public courses through apps like Apple's iTunesU. They have everything from language arts to biology, from law and politics to behavioral economics. Other great places to check out are websites like Open Learn and Open Learning Initiative, where you can pick and choose from hundreds of free courses.

Another solid choice would be a website like Coursera. It isn't free, but for a fraction of the cost of going to college and floundering, you can test the waters of different majors. You may end up finding out you have an interest in something you'd never considered.

Forge Ahead—The Path of Service

Another form of non-traditional education is joining AmeriCorps, which is a national civil society program that involves intensive community service. Programs usually last around 10 months with about two weeks of training at the beginning. Another option is the Peace Corps, which is a international volunteer program. Some jobs in the program require a college degree, but not all. They will give you three months of training before sending you on your assignment, which usually lasts two years.

These organizations will allow you to travel to other parts of the country and world. Joining either of these agencies will give you amazing opportunities to do service work of varying degrees—and build strengths that will make you desirable to potential employers. You won't make a ton of money, but you won't need to. You'll be able to live on very little since you won't have already racked up a bunch of debt.

In an article published by The Aspen Institute, a panel talks about all the beneficial qualities someone has after spending time in either AmeriCorps or the Peace Corps. Here are a few of the ones they listed:

- Mission Oriented
- Globally Minded
- Leadership Experience
- Flexible
- Collaborative
- Exceptional Intercultural Skills

Don't go into either of these programs thinking they are going to be easy. You'll need to be very dedicated and committed to whatever cause they assign you. Be prepared to put in hard work and long hours. You'll learn a lot about yourself, and have firsthand experience interacting with other cultures. You'll learn the realities of how other people live outside of American privilege, which is more than your peers will be learning in the classroom.

Grab Your Passport and Ship Out

The last thing anyone encourages you to do when you're getting ready to graduate high school is take off around the world...but why not take off on an adventure? I've found traveling to be the most rewarding kind of education. All you'll need to do is save up a couple grand (which should be easy since you're probably still living at home and you have no debt). I struggled to save for my trip to Italy because I was already juggling school debt and the cost of living on my own. If you're starting with a blank slate, it should be a cake walk to save the money you need. You'll also need to get a passport, pick a destination, and buy a plane ticket.

Australia is a great place to go if you're between the ages of 18 and 27 (they have a young vibe in their country). They have a lot of employment programs specifically for backpackers and transient workers. You can work odd jobs in any country, like being an English-speaking tour guide or waiting tables in a café, to fund your travels. Be creative and use websites like couchsurfing.net to find hostels and other cheap or even free places to stay. Sometimes you can find a gig working at a hostel for free room and board. Not too shabs! Stay open to meeting new friends and learning something from each person; these connections will add so much richness to your journey! I know the idea of traveling alone can be terrifying, but the world isn't nearly as scary as many lesser-traveled people think.

I learned more about myself in the months I spent exploring Italy than I did in the entire year I spent trying to do the "college thing." I wish I would have had the forethought to travel after high school. It's the perfect time. Once you've made the decision to take off and travel the world, many people will look at you like you're crazy, but don't let that stop you. If the idea of traveling lights you up and starts a fire in your belly, you need to go. Start a blog while you're traveling and document everything. Who knows, maybe you'll end up getting paid for it!

Think outside the box when it comes to your education. Don't let fear cause you to settle for a path that doesn't suit you. If college doesn't feel right, don't go. It doesn't mean you're lazy; it means your mind is open and your eyes are set on finding a different way. College will always be there waiting if you decide that's your bliss. Seeing the world, expanding your horizons and experiencing life from other people's perspectives is going to give you the kind of education you'll never experience in a classroom. It alters your life and changes the paradigm of your thinking.

How you'll get an education is one of the most important decisions you'll make. The idea is to shift what getting an education looks like. You're living during a time when every piece of information you could possibly want to know is right at your fingertips. There's no excuse for living ignorantly, naively, or lazily. If you don't know where to start, a quick online search can help get your mind moving and guide you to action. There are individuals out there who are already doing what you want to do, or something similar. Find them, ask questions, and make them your teachers. Use your resources and think outside the box. You're in charge 20-Something: let the education you choose be what lights you up and guides you into awareness.

Chapter Eight
FOR THE LOVE OF MONEY

"If you can cut a check for the problem, you don't have that problem."

- Dean Graziosi

Writing this chapter is comical for me. As I was polishing previous chapters, inching closer every day to writing this one, I was apprehensive. How in God's name am I going to give anyone advice about money? I have been notoriously irresponsible with my finances for years—teetering between barely getting all (okay, most) of my bills paid, and total financial ruin. Living paycheck to paycheck is a stressful art form.

The only real success I've had financially during my 20s has been not over-drafting my account more than a handful of times, and I've always paid my rent on time. You learn to appreciate the little victories when your income doesn't look like Steve Job's. Yet somehow, I've managed to take a bunch of fun vacations, and I have plenty of nice things to show for all the hard work I've done. Unfortunately, I also have about $9k in credit card debt to show for it, too. Ah, well, can you really put a price tag on life experiences and fond memories? I think not. Many people would probably disagree, which is why I've gathered some great advice for you (and really for me, too) from a savvy financial coach named Ericka Young.

Starting Off on the Right Foot

Right out of high school you're going to be forced to make decisions that will set the tone for the next decade of your life (at least). You'll need money whether you're choosing a four-year college, an associate program, a technical school, or traveling. Taking on student loans to pay for your education is as natural as breathing these days, but it shouldn't be. Ericka says, "If your school costs $40k per year, you shouldn't have more than $20k in loans." That means you're going to need to figure out how to pay for the rest without borrowing money from a bank.

Enter: community college. I know you're excited about finally being done with high school and becoming this awesome, independent person... but trust me, you have plenty of years to become fully independent.

According to the National Center for Education Statistics, only 58 percent of undergrads at public universities graduate within six years. I don't know about you, but I have zero interest in acquiring six years' worth of student loan debt. If you decide to get a master's degree, or are going to medical or law school, you're looking at 10+ years of debt, and interest! Oh, I shudder. Spending the first few years getting your prerequisite classes out of the way at a community college will save you thousands of dollars. Getting a job and covering some of your tuition while you're in school isn't easy, but it will be insanely rewarding when it comes time to start paying back loans.

If you have the option to live at home while you're going to school, do it. I know you're tired of being under your parents' roof, but it's a big expensive world out there and adding living expenses on top of your education is only going to make things harder. You have an entire lifetime after college to be on your own. If living at home isn't an option, find roommates. Pick the cheapest apartment you can find and share the expenses with two or three other people. Roommates can be annoying, but you'll save money and it will be a great learning experience. Also, when the time comes that you get to live on your own, you'll have a deeper appreciation for the clean, quiet space that is all yours.

Do whatever you can during your time in school to come out with as little debt as possible. Millennials have a collective debt of trillions of dollars. Yes, I said trillions. Don't join the debt club if you can avoid it. I went through one year of college and 11 months of cosmetology school and came out nearly $50k in debt. I wish I had worked during those two years to lighten the load of that debt, but I didn't. I worked, but only so I had money to live. Otherwise, I lived off of my loans; it was easy, and I was having a good time. Hey, it's all fun and games until you start getting hefty bills in the mail immediately after graduation.

Before you're done with school, learn how much your loan payments are going to be: this is not something you want to be surprised about. If you had to take out more than one student loan, start researching consolidation; one payment is easier to make than four (I know this from experience).

I Have a Grown-up Job. Now What?

Congrats 20-Something, you're done with school and you finally have your first real job and a steady paycheck! It's an exciting time. You want to have fun and do all the things you're supposed to be doing in your 20s like partying and traveling. By all means do those things. Just remember, having fun for too long and not taking into account the important things can be devastating to your bank account. Financial Coach Ericka said it best: "We need to find balance." She understands that 20-Somethings don't always like the word "budget," that it can feel restrictive and uncomfortable. I've always been afraid that a budget would cause me to see my level of broke-ness in black and white, and once I couldn't hide from it it, I'd never get to have any fun. Ericka laughed warmly and assured me this wouldn't be the case. "Budgets create the framework you need so that your finances don't feel so scattered and unreliable." Okay, Ericka, fair enough. Listen up, 20-Somethings: you need a budget (and so do I).

Ericka and I compiled a list of eight important things to accomplish in your 20s.

1. **Have Fun and Enjoy Your Money, But Don't Let it Get Out of Hand.**

    - How often are you partying? Maybe instead of every weekend, you should limit yourself to once or twice a month. I know this might seem impossible, but think of all the money and calories you'll save! Also, drinking with friends at home is a fraction of the cost!

    - How often are you shopping? I know Target shopping sprees are wildly addicting, but planning to spend $50 and coming out $200 poorer isn't a sustainable habit. Make a list before entering the black hole that is Target and only get what's on your list. I know it's hard, but I believe in you.

    - Traveling: by now you know how I feel about traveling (it's a must-do), but do it responsibly. Plan your trips in advance, save for them, and be creative about how you travel. Do things as cheaply as possible. Find hostels, or free places to stay, eat inexpensively and if you can, take advantage of bike shares or plan to walk a lot. Traveling doesn't have to break the bank, and the savvier you become, the more trips you'll be able to take.

2. **Get Out of Debt.**
   (student loans and credit cards)

   - Get creative with how you bring in income. Uber anyone? Sell those college textbooks.

   - Utiliz e your freedom. Chances are, you don't have a family of your own yet, or a mortgage, so if you need to take on a second job, you have the space to do it. Direct sales companies such as Beachbody, It Works!, Mary Kay and Younique allow you to work from home, building your own little franchise, on your own schedule. You just need to have social media connections and a few networking skills, and you'll be up and running in no time. I have a lot of friends who work for those companies, and they love it. It's an easy way to supplement income (and many people make enough money to end up doing it full-time).

3. **Learn How to Live on Your Own.**

- Live modestly. Earlier I suggested having roommates in college; the same also goes for after. Maybe you have one roommate instead of three now, but having someone to share expenses will help ease the burden. I shared my first apartment with one of my girlfriends, and after the initial period of learning each other's habits (she hates leaving lights on, I hate windows being left open when we're not home), we had a blast living together. We had our own separate friends—and lives—but we also had each other. We became our own little family during that time.

- Don't buy a fancy car. I got a car when I was 17 and I've been driving it for the past 11 years. Of course,, it would be great to have a newer, nicer car—to pull up to valet parking at luxury hotels in something other than my less-than-pristine 2005 Hyundai Elantra with the Hello Kitty window decal. But, a pricy car payment might mean I'm not able to stay at that fine hotel. Sometimes you have to pick and choose where you're going to be fancy...until you've made your millions, that is.

4. **Start Saving for Retirement.**

- I know retirement is the furthest thing from our minds as 20-Somethings, but it shouldn't be. If we start adding even small amounts of money to a retirement fund now, we can easily save over a million dollars by the time we are ready to retire. It's critical to set up a fund now and let the money accrue.

- Take advantage of company matching programs with your 401k and retirement funds. A lot of companies will match a percentage of the money you contribute to your retirement savings account. If your company offers this, do it: it's free money!

5. **Don't Get Financially Attached to Other People.**

- If you come from a situation where you always had to work for what you wanted, this should be a breeze for you. But if your parents were able to buy you everything you wanted, as well as pay all your bills, this concept might be tougher to swallow. It's critical that you know how to pay your own way in this world. What will happen when the money train inevitably stops and for the first time, you are bearing the weight of all your own bills? Start taking control of your money. This goes for how you split costs with roommates and significant others, too. It's one thing to share expenses; it's a whole other thing for someone else to be paying for everything. Learn how to be independent.

6. **Have Conversations with Financial Professionals and Insurance Agents so You Don't Make Stupid Mistakes.**

    - People love a pro-active 20-Something who is inquisitive and wants to do better. It's easier to guide young people instead of correcting 20 years of bad financial practice.

7. **Credit Card Risks.**

    - It's good to have a credit card to start establishing your credit score, but be very careful and don't let your spending get out of control.

    - Whenever you buy something (non-emergency) with your credit card, make sure you're able to pay it off at the end of each month. I can tell you from firsthand experience, credit card spending is a slippery slope.

8. **Don't Rush into Home Ownership.**

    - Owning a home can have enormous costs. When you're the owner, you're responsible for everything that goes wrong: leaky roof, malfunctioning water heater, sewage issues, broken windows, fallen trees. You have to pay property taxes and homeowners' insurance premiums. Renting might not be an "investment" like buying can be, but you aren't responsible for fixing things when they break. You also have the ability to move and change your living situation at will.

- Just because you could be paying the same monthly fee on a mortgage that you are on rent, doesn't mean you should buy. Don't let anyone fool you into thinking that home ownership is always worth the investment. Interest alone can double the cost of home ownership over the term of the mortgage. If you pay $200k for a home on a 30 year mortgage, you'll end up paying $400k in the long run. Not to mention paying around $2k in processing fees when you buy, and 6% realty commissions when you go to sell. Whenever someone suggests I buy something when they find out how much I pay in rent, I say, "no thanks!" I'd much rather take all that money and travel the world. Proceed with caution, friend.

A Few Final Pointers

If you're struggling to stay on top of your bills, look for ways to decrease your spending. Do you really need that Starbucks coffee with a double shot? Or could you start making coffee at home?

If you want a gym membership, find the least expensive gym in your area and join, even if it isn't the fanciest. Every time you're going to whip out that debit card, assess whether you NEED whatever it is you're about to buy, or whether you simply WANT it. Take it from a recovering "want" buyer, going without wants for now is going to pay off big time.

Sometimes, phone, cable and Internet companies are willing to negotiate pricing. Don't be afraid to call and confidently ask about lowering your monthly fees. You'd be shocked at what companies are willing to do when you tell them you'll be moving your business elsewhere because you found cheaper rates. Someone can always give you a better deal; you just have to be talking to the right person.

Do your financial legwork now, 20-Something. Your 30-Something self will thank you. You'll be walking into the next decade with your eyes wide open, and with any luck, more money in your wallet.

Chapter Nine
LIVING FEARLESSLY

"Becoming fearless isn't the point. That's impossible. It's learning how to control your fear, and how to be free from it."

— Veronica Roth, Divergent

Learning to be brave in the face of fear is one of the best ways to know what freedom feels like. It is the key to taking control of your thoughts and feelings, and manifesting everything you've ever wanted. There will be countless times in your life when fear tries to immobilize you. Look that fear in the face and say, "You don't control me!"

Being fearless doesn't mean you're not afraid of anything; it means you recognize what you're afraid of, and you've developed the courage to work through it. Part of fearless living is identifying the things that could possibly go wrong, but because you've declared success as your only option, you power on. It's beautiful when you can look at something that didn't turn out the way you thought it would and still see all the amazing outcomes that came from doing it.

Failure is a state of mind, and much like any other thought or belief, you can change it. I thought I had met the love of my life. We seemed to be on the path to marriage. I did everything I thought was right, but in the end, it wasn't enough. A weaker version of Ronni would've seen it as a failure. However, 2017 Ronni sees how many lessons I learned over the course of our relationship. I don't feel that our nearly two years together was a failure at all. We helped elevate each other. He was exactly what I needed during that chapter of my life. And, even though it ended in a heap of lies and betrayal, I regret nothing.

Bravery and Courage are life partners. Bravery is strong and domineering. She forces you to take notice of fear, even when you'd rather ignore it. She calls upon Courage to act. When Courage succeeds, she strengthens Bravery's ability to act again next time. Courage is the little voice in your head that tells you to keep trying even when you're terrified. Fear will creep in; it will test your resolve, it will try to plant seeds of doubt. But when Bravery and Courage get together, they give birth to Strength. They set up a veritable fortress around your heart and mind.

11 Times You've Been Afraid and Didn't Know It

1. **When you were leaving home for the first time**
   It's a big scary world out there. Of course, you were afraid when you finally left the nest. I was nervous when I left for college, but I went anyway. It's normal to be a little fearful of the unknown. But, you swallowed that lump in your throat and stepped over the threshold into adulthood. Go, you!

2. **When you finally met someone worth falling in love with**
   People are afraid of love for many reasons. Maybe it's because of previous heartbreak, or because of not growing up in a loving environment. Whatever the reason, the concept of love can be foreign. Falling in love, whether you've done it before or not, is beautiful. Don't let fear taint something that has the power to bring so much joy to your being.

3. **When you looked at your bank account**
   That moment of dread when you knew the responsible thing to do was check your bank account balance, but suddenly you found yourself in fight-or-flight mode. We've all been there. Don't worry, you're not broke: you're just Millennial broke. You have a roof over your head, some amount of food in your fridge, you went out for drinks last night and probably bought a new shirt last weekend. So what if you're within cents of over-drafting your account? Your next paycheck will come through in a few days. You'll survive.

4. **When you quit your job**
   Maybe you quit because you decided to take a leap of faith and go do something totally new and different. Perhaps it's because you hated where you worked and wanted to go do whatever it is you do, somewhere else. Whatever the reason, replace that fear with excitement. Leaving a toxic work environment will only lead to awesomeness!

5. **When you traveled alone for the first time**
   If you've traveled alone, you know that feeling of fear mixed with exhilaration. It can be scary to venture into unknown territories alone, but my guess is that since you decided to travel alone in the first place, you're already well on your way to mastering the art of fearlessness.

6. **When you broke up with your first love**
   Even if you're the one who ended things, it's still scary. What if I don't find another person to love me? What if he/she really is the one, but I'm just not seeing the bigger picture? Quit living in the "what if" scenarios and embrace what is. If the relationship isn't bringing you joy, it's time to move on. You're opening yourself up to find someone who lights a fire in your soul, and with any luck, your loins, too.

7. **When you broke up with your best friend**

   As someone who takes her friendships very seriously, I know the tragedy that comes with breaking up with a best friend. It's heart wrenching. You're afraid you'll never have another friend who knows you as well, or who you'll connect with as deeply. Fear not: if you're walking away from this person, it's probably because he or she no longer serves a positive purpose in your life. Friendships come with no lifetime guarantee, and it's OK to let go of the ones that have soured.

8. **When you had to decide which job to take**

   You were afraid you might make a mistake and choose the wrong job. Maybe you were even paralyzed by having to make such a big decision. Job offers don't come along every day, and suddenly you found yourself faced with multiple options. You thought, What if I choose wrong? When your anxiety is casting a shadow of doubt over your gut instinct, make a "pros" and "cons" list. If you still can't decide, flip a coin and let fate decide.

9. **When you bought your first "big ticket" item**
My first big-ticket item was a couch for my first apartment. I paid around $600 for it. I was pretty terrified. WHAT IF I GO BROKE? What if I don't like it after a week? I've had these feelings multiple other times when purchasing an expensive item. What I can tell you is that you likely won't go broke. But if you're that afraid, maybe you should hold off.

10. **When someone you love died**
Losing loved ones is devastating. Suddenly they're no longer around for you to call, hang out with, or catch up with. Living without their guidance can cause a lot of fear. How will I ever function without them? But how can you not try? My guess is, they wouldn't want you to stop living. With everything you do, honor them. Live a

fuller life for them. There's grief when you lose someone you love, but being afraid of their absence will only hold you back.

11. **When your beliefs were challenged**

    We were all raised with certain belief systems, and not everyone will agree with yours. The first time someone questioned yours, did you get a little annoyed? Angry, even? It was probably because you were afraid. Having your beliefs challenged, when you're not ready for them to be questioned, or when you can't really explain why you believe what you believe, will trigger fear. What if everything you've ever been taught doesn't match who you want to be, or who you are? If you no longer believe the same way your family does, will they still love you? Will you still love yourself? Will you be able to recognize yourself under the veil of different beliefs? The truth is, questioning your beliefs is a natural part of life, and the evolution of them is necessary for personal growth.

I'm Attached to My Arms, Not My Ideas

Everyone has preconceived ideas of how things should be. I blame our culture. There are expectations set when we're young and then we beat ourselves up if we aren't living up to these specific expectations. We think we should be doing things a certain way because that's how we succeed—by following established principles.

There was a time I had certain ideas about my self-worth. Most of my life, my ego was telling me that if other people needed me, it made me important. I needed to be needed. Lord, have mercy.

From a young age, I was what my mom lovingly referred to as the "Dear Abby" of my friends (in reference to the newspaper columnist who offered advice to her readers' problems.).

I always wondered why people felt compelled to talk to me about their issues—especially when they were way out of my range of expertise.

A friend recently helped shed light on this: "You're a fantastic listener. You have this unbelievable ability to listen and take in anyone's problems and not judge them." Hmmm...I hadn't ever thought about it like that, and while I'm glad I have the ability to do this, I also know I need to be mindful of how I allow it to affect my life.

The trouble is, I had a habit of turning other people's problems into my own. I think women in general tend to do this. We try so hard to be there for our girlfriends, significant others, and just about everyone in between...to be the empathetic creatures we're meant to be, that suddenly our (un)happiness seems to align perfectly with theirs. They are in crisis/we are in crisis. It's like we're programmed to do this. I did it for a long time.

Until I let go of the idea that I needed to be needed, my happiness ebbed and flowed with my friends and loved ones. It's exhausting to think about now.

6 Ideals Worth Changing

1. **THE TIME**

    "Holy cow, I can't believe I slept until noon! Ugh, I'm so lazy," or, "Jeez, it's 4 o'clock already and I still haven't started writing that paper yet. Why can't I get my shit together?" One of the things being a writer has taught me is that time is a fluid concept. Who cares if you slept until noon on your day off? Seriously, who is suffering because of your extra sleep? Who cares if you didn't start doing anything productive until late afternoon? Just because other people are up at dawn to start their day doesn't mean you need to be. Personally, I function much better at night. I stay up late, even when I have to get up early. We don't all have to function on the same timetable. As long as you're meeting deadlines, who cares when you do things?

2. **WEIGHT**
    You hold this idea that you need to maintain a certain weight, and as long as you do, you'll be happy. How about this: maintain a healthy weight so you don't run out of breath going up and down the stairs. Reach whatever fitness goals you want to set for yourself, and stop feeling like you need to be running marathons and joining Beach Body like everyone on your newsfeed (unless that's your goal, in which case, go you!). Stop comparing your weight to everyone else's. Comparison is were happiness goes to die.

3. **FINANCES**
    So you feel like you should have a certain amount of money in your checking and savings accounts. You're attached to the idea that making more money than you're making is how you'll be happy. If you're fiscally irrespon-

sible, do something about that, but don't expect more money to equal more happiness. Learn to be happy right now, earning whatever it is you're earning, and when more money comes to you, you'll know how to really appreciate it. If you learn how to manage money properly, you'll realize living comfortably doesn't require a fortune. Unless your life goal is to drive a Rolls-Royce and live in a rooftop penthouse in Paris. Then, yes, perhaps you do need to make a fortune.

4. **RELATIONSHIPS**

    We hold tightly onto ideals of what relationships should look like and how they should progress. The reality is that every relationship needs space and time to grow and evolve. One couple might be together for a year and decide to get married. Another couple might be together for five years and still not be ready for marriage. One couple might decide they're ready for a baby, even though they aren't married, and they have a baby. Another couple might be married and never have children because it's not for them. There is no "supposed to" when it comes to relationships. Stop comparing yours to someone else's. The more time you spend trying to fit your relationship into some perfect box, the less time you're spending enjoying the relationship. Instead of letting it blossom, you're going to stifle it until it dies.

5. **CAREER SUCCESS**

    Like relationships, careers progress in their own way and time. Some people manage to find their dream job early on, and to everyone watching, they are crushing it. They're climbing the corporate ladder and stepping over anybody in their way. Good for them! For other people, it might take longer to find a niche, or to find a career path that really sticks. Take your time. The absolute death of progress is spending time comparing yourself to everyone on your Facebook feed.

6. **WHAT IS VS. WHAT ISN'T**
   You've got to learn to embrace the is-ness of a situation. You might say, "I don't want to have such a small amount of money in my bank account. I hate it." I understand that; I hate it, too. But the more time you spend beating yourself up, the less time you have to figure out a way to make it better. The sooner you accept the is-ness, the faster you'll find a solution. The more time you spend focusing on what you don't have, or what isn't there (like more money), the longer it will take you to find a solution.

Ego vs. Higher Self (or God, If That's Your Thing)

Who doesn't have a little asshole voice in their head that tries to stifle their progress in life? That's your ego talking. I'm telling you, we all have one. She's really good at trying to sabotage us and make us feel like imposters. She's the one who tries to hit the panic button when all we need is to stay calm.

Fearlessness and Courage come from your higher self (or God, Allah, or the Holy Mother, depending on your belief system). She is the zen voice in your head, the one who tells you everything is going to be okay, even if you can't see how that's possible. She's the one who provides a sense of calm when ego is stirring up chaos.

Ego is driven by fear and doubt, while your Higher Self is driven by love, trust and gratitude. Love and fear cannot coexist. In order to connect to your Higher Self, you have to let go of that fear and silence that doubt. This won't happen all at once; it's a practice. It's a decision you make right now, and every day you work toward it.

Ego Says,

"You better be worried about that bill coming up. Where's the money going to come from?"

Higher Self Says,

"Everything always works out. Things will come together. I'm alive, I'm okay."

Ego Says,

"Don't trust anyone. Be hesitant. Keep yourself closed off so you don't get hurt again."

Higher Self Says,

"You've been hurt in the past, but your ability to continue to love and trust is beautiful. Never hold yourself back from experiencing the joy life has in store or you. Remain open to receive it."

Are you getting the gist? The idea is catching yourself in a negative thought and immediately changing it into a positive...even if you can't see how you're going to get from A to B.

You Are What You Think

One major key to learning to be fearless is recognizing the power of your own thoughts. What if I told you that you're completely in control of your feelings? Do you agree, or does it make you immediately start thinking about all the times when you didn't believe you were in control of them? Well, I'm telling you, you're in control of your own thoughts, your own feelings, and your own happiness. You can't always control the outcome of a situation, but you can control how you react to it. You can't control how other people act, but you can control how they make you feel. Learning to take responsibility for your thoughts, feelings and actions is imperative.

5 Steps to Zen:

1. **You Are Not a Victim.**
   Living life with a victim mentality is a quick route to misery. You are not the

victim of your circumstances. If your circumstances aren't changing, maybe it is because you think you're a victim. Victims don't take action, they don't act; they react. Take responsibility for the choices you've made that have brought you to where you are. Take my debt, for instance: I chose to go to college, so now I have student loan debt to pay back. Of course,, I don't enjoy having to shell out money each month for those loans, but I made the choice to take them on so I could go to school. I'm not a victim of our expensive education system. I could've taken another path, but that's the one I chose.

Maybe you feel like a victim because someone was mean to you, or treated you unfairly, or maybe you had crappy parents and feel like you got raw end of the deal. Buck up soldier, you're no victim. You hold all the power to change your circumstances. Of course,, things are going to happen sometimes that aren't palatable;

they'll probably even piss you off, but that's life. If you allow negative things that happen to penetrate your soul and cause you to walk around angry and resentful, the only person hurting you is you. What total misery to live a life where happiness is only as good as the last thing someone did to you. Which brings me to step 2...

2. **Don't Take Anything Personally.**

   Have you ever stopped during a fit of road rage to consider that the person isn't being an asshole driver because he or she hates you? Someone's poor driving habits aren't a personal slam to you. My road rage generally consists of random outbursts of, "douchebag!" and, "what are you even doing right now!" Occasionally I'll lob an F-bomb or two. The thing is, I don't think that person is actually a douchebag, I just think he's driving like one. I'm sure he's a perfectly lovely person, but in that moment, his driving is making me want to get out of my car and start kicking his. I also know that there are plenty of times someone was probably yelling "douchebag" at me. We're all shitty drivers now and then (some more than others). I've found that the more I admit to my own shortcomings, the more tolerable other people's shortcomings are to me.

When I decided it was time to quit Salon B, my boss immediately flipped a switch in her brain. One side of the switch was the me she loved and adored, and the other side was the me who had to make a decision she didn't like. She reduced me to a single decision I made, and with that, she decided she didn't know me at all. She called me names, and threw every nice thing she'd ever done for me back in my face. I know I'm not all the things she called me after I decided to leave. I know I'm not all the things she told other people I am. Her reaction had everything to do with her, and nothing to do with me. If I took everything she did personally, it would be devastating to my heart and mind. It would also be pointless, because I know who I am, and if she could remove her anger, disappointment and ego, she'd remember who I am, too. I have moved forward, still knowing who I am.

You have to do the same. Other people's reactions to you are about them, not you. This doesn't give you license to go around being a dick, and there will be times when you owe people an apology. But, when you're trying to live your best life, you'll have to make choices that piss people off. The key is, if these people are really your tribe, they won't take it personally.

3. **Be Secure in Who You Are.**

If you don't know who you are, then your love and acceptance of self will ebb and flow with other people's love for, and acceptance of, you. If I ask you who you are, and your answer starts with, "Well people have said I'm fill in the blank," does that mean you won't be that thing anymore once those people change their mind about you? For example, if you say, "People have said I'm down to earth." Okay, great. First of all, what does that even mean and why does everyone start their personality profile with it? Second, if the next person who comes along says you're not down to earth, does that change whether or not you actually are? If I ask you who you are, I'm not asking who other people think you are, I'm asking who you know you are based on no one's opinion but your own. Have you ever considered the difference?

Always know your own worth, and stand strong in what you believe. You are not the sum total of how someone else defines you. There are people in this world who will try to fit you into a box; it's their attempt to define you. The stronger and more unique you are, the harder they will try to extinguish your flame. To know who you are is threatening to people who are lost. Don't be afraid to stand alone sometimes, in the name of your own truth. Sometimes you will have to do the unpopular thing, or forge a path less known. Do it! Those are the things leaders do. When you stand with a strong sense of self, you will not be rocked by anyone, or anything, around you. You'll be able to see and appreciate the beauty in every scenario. Where other people see obstacles you will see adventure. In Brené Brown's book, Braving the Wilderness, she talks about the importance of staying true to who you are. She refers to this vulnerable place as the Wilderness. It can be terrifying, but it's where our most authentic selves reside.

4. **Accept People for Who They Are, Not Who You Want Them To Be.**
One major key to why so many relationships fail, is because one person is projecting their own feelings onto the other person. They want the other person to be someone they aren't. When they can't get them to

act the way they think they should act, all is lost. Don't try to force people to be something they're not. Thinking you know what's better for others than they do is presumptuous and downright rude. Do you get annoyed when someone thinks you should do something differently than how you're doing it? There are a thousand different ways to get from A to B. Yours isn't necessarily the best way but it's also not likely the worst. I don't expect others to change the essence of who they are simply because I don't like it or agree with it.

You're not going to like or agree with every person you meet. What a boring world it would be otherwise. I can accept you for who you are, but that doesn't mean I want you in my life, and that is a two-way street. Don't be all butt-hurt when someone doesn't want you in his or her life. It doesn't diminish how awesome you are. You are not the sum total of everyone's opinion of you.

5. **Your Inner Peace is Your Responsibility.** How often do you find yourself thinking or saying, "I'll be so happy when, fill in the blank," immediately putting the state of your peace and happiness in the hands of a circumstance. Are you going to finally be happy when you lose those last 10 pounds? How about when you finally start making more money? When the debt is gone? When your significant other starts treating you better? What is your "I'll be happier when..." statement? We all have one. I'll tell you what: things will be better when you take control of your life and stop letting your circumstances control you. Stop waiting around to be happy. Embrace who you are, and what is, right now. Before you know it, you won't have to try to find inner peace, you'll have it.

The better you get at controlling your ego and the thoughts that run through your head, the more inner peace you'll have. The more inner peace you have, the faster you're going to be able to master the art of manifestation. Everything you've ever wanted can be yours: all you have to do is ask, and believe it will happen.

Know What You Want? Manifest That Shit.

When you want something, ask for it, and then take actions as though you're within moments of getting what you asked for. Everything that's happening in my life right now, I've manifested. It didn't happen overnight, and it hasn't always looked exactly how I thought it would, but it happened, and I'm living it.

> Declaring your intent
> + Actions
> + Faith
> = Results.

I want to go over the difference between being optimistic and pessimistic and why it's important to be an optimist.

Optimistic:
adjective
1.
disposed to take a favorable view of events or conditions and to expect the most favorable outcome.

Pessimistic:
adjective
1.
pertaining to or characterized by pessimism or the tendency to expect only bad outcomes; gloomy; joyless; unhopeful.

Being an optimist doesn't mean you don't recognize the possibility of bad things happening; it means you don't expect bad things to happen. Optimists expect things to go well, and generally, they do. It's called the power of positive thinking. Pessimists (who I call Eeyores) expect bad things to happen. You can't manifest awesomeness in your life if you're an Eeyore. You can't ask to have more money show up in your life, and then expect not to get it. It doesn't work that way.

Eeyores talk about what they don't want to have happen. Optimists talk about what they do want.

Eyore: "I don't want to get another bill in the mail. I can't afford it."

Optimist: "I want money to start coming to me from unexpected places."

If you're not used to this, it might seem crazy at first. "You're telling me, all I have to do is say things differently and then I'll get what I want?" Yes. That's exactly what I'm saying. It's all about your frame of mind. Say what you want out loud. Repeat it. Close your eyes and make yourself feel how it will feel when it happens. Remind yourself every day of what you're working toward and you'll automatically start walking toward it. It's like throwing a football: in order to throw successfully at your target, you have to be looking at your target, not at the ball. Keep your eye on where you're going.

Eyore: "I don't want another relationship like the last one. I keep picking the same type of guys."

Optimist: "I want to find a relationship that adds to my happiness and elevates my life. One where I feel safe to be myself and can love freely and be loved wholly."

During my five adult years of singledom, there were a lot of times I thought I was ready for a relationship, but when someone would ask me what I wanted in a partner, I could only think of what I didn't want. The more you talk about what you don't want to have happen, the more likely it is to happen. I had a lot of trouble coming up with anything of substance that I wanted in someone, but no trouble saying what I didn't want. Oddly enough, I kept finding what I didn't want.

Slowly I started changing my thought process, and with each new date, I started getting closer to finding what I wanted. About six months before I met Mr. Wonderful, I wrote a list of things I wanted to find in someone. As I focused on that list, I felt my heart opening. I felt more ready than ever to be in a relationship and to be able to give myself to that relationship.

Your ego is going to hate this positive thinking game. Your ego is going to say, "This is stupid. This is so unrealistic. You're not going to change anything by sitting here talking out loud to yourself, idiot." You have to tell your ego to shove it, and keep going. Your ego is a real douche and is not to be obeyed.

Remind yourself often of your goals and desires. Think about something you've wanted so badly but have always been too afraid to ask for—then ask for it. Remember, we're living fearlessly now. There's nothing too big for the universe to give you. Money, love, a new job, vacations, whatever it is, speak about it, feel it, and stay open to receive it. This, my friends, is the Law of Attraction. This is what I'm talking about when I say I have manifested all the amazing things that are happening in my life. I spoke and the universe listened.

When I wanted to change my hours at Salon B to part-time, I didn't know what I would do with the time I was freeing for myself; all I had was the distinct feeling that I needed to make the space. When the part-time plan blew up in my face, I had the distinct feeling that I needed to walk away, so I did. I didn't have a plan, I just listened to my instincts—the voice of my higher self. If I had let my ego creep in, I might've made the mistake of staying, and I'd still be struggling a year later.

Immediately things started falling into place when I left Salon B. I got the job at Salon C right away. I was able to go part-time within a few months and to hand-pick the exact schedule I wanted, and then the opportunity to write this book fell in my lap. That's how I know I've gotten good at manifesting, because one thing after another keeps going right. That's not to say nothing negative ever happens, it absolutely does. But, going with the flow is much easier now that I'm not trying to resist every plot twist.

There is no limit on what you can achieve when you start connecting with your higher self. "Ask and you shall receive" will become your life motto. Anyone who doubts you (including your ego), let them know, "I'm on a journey to live my fullest life. Either get on board or get out of my way."

The longer you've lived in discontent and unhappiness, the more difficult it's going to be to adopt this practice. If you've grown up in an environment where the motto is struggle, always struggle, it's going to be hard for you to break through that programmed thinking—but you can do it. I believe in you. Life doesn't have to be so hard. I believe in your ability to make significant changes to impact your future. It doesn't matter what happened to you before this; it doesn't matter what mistakes you made or what people did to you. Now is the time to let it go. It's not your story anymore. It's something that happened, but it's not going to define the rest of your life.

Peace Out

I wanted to leave you with the image of me sitting in a fluffy white bathrobe, on the balcony of a suite at the Ritz-Carlton in Grand Cayman. I wanted to tell you how surreal it felt to be there, watching the waves crash, feeling the salty air on my face, and listening as the love of my life moved about inside our room, preparing for the day's adventures. I wanted to leave you with how incredible it felt to have found myself in such a beautiful place with someone who loved and adored me. But I cannot do that. While that did happen once, it's not the real ending to this story.

Instead, I find myself standing alone on the side of a mountain in Utah, where I came to escape my realities back home. As I stare out over the vastness of the mountain ranges surrounding me, I have to remind myself to breathe. "Mr. Wonderful" turned out to be anything but. The heartbreak is real. It is gritty and intense. I'd give anything to numb the hurricane of emotions churning inside of me, but I will face it head-on. It's important to feel, 20-Something. It's important to lean into those feelings, even when you're shaking from head to toe.

As the last chapter of this book comes to an end, so, too, does this chapter in my life. What you and I do from here is wildly important. Will we put to use all of the lessons in this book? Or, will we ignore them and spend the next decade constantly tripping over our own two feet? Who am I kidding? I'll do that anyway. Will you?

If I have one hope for us, it is that we dive fully into the depths of our psyches, no matter how dark and scary it feels, and wade around long enough to find our truest, most authentic selves. Don't run from yourself, 20-Something. You're far too strong for that.

Sometimes people turn out to be different than we thought they were...and things don't work out the way we hoped they would. Sometimes our hearts hurt so much it's hard to breathe. But the more gracefully you let go, the more beautiful life will be. Let go of things and people not meant for you. The more willing you are to do this, the more intimately you will get to know yourself, and the happier you'll be. As you get out of your own way and learn to live wholeheartedly, you'll be surrounded by others who reflect this back at you. What I have learned throughout my 20s is that the more I got out of my own way, the more content I became. My intuition always knows better than I do about what should happen next. My life is way cooler than I could've ever planned, had I been holding on tightly to some ridiculous ideal of how it should be.

We are powerful and strong, 20-Something. Just the same as I believe in my own strength and resiliency, I believe in yours. Embrace all the unknowns. Find excitement in all the things you have left to learn, and all the adventures you're going to have discovering the answers.

So, this is where I leave you. You are ready to take on the world. Remember, you're more in charge than you think.
Take control of those thoughts, ask for what you want, put into question ideas that are holding you back, kick your Eeyore tendencies to the curb, and get ready for the universe to rain blessings down on you like springtime in Chicago.
Leave your umbrella behind and let them soak through you. Go enjoy the big, messy, beautiful adventure ahead of you.

Love Ronni x

About the Author

Ronni Morgan is the owner of Breakup with Ronni, a coaching and consulting service where she works with clients through break-ups. Not only with significant others, but breakups with anything holding her clients back from reaching their goals. Ronni built and sold a successful hair salon in Indianapolis, Indiana before ultimately choosing to sell it, and go explore the world for a while. She hates talking about herself in the 3rd person almost as much as she hates small talk, and lives for getting real with people, in order to get to the bottom of their self-limiting beliefs.

Check her out on Facebook and Instagram
@RonniMorgan.

www.ingramcontent.com/pod-product-compliance
Lightning Source LLC
Chambersburg PA
CBHW071913290426
44110CB00013B/1368